HAUNTED
ILLINOIS

SECOND EDITION

HAUNTED ILLINOIS

GHOSTS AND STRANGE PHENOMENA OF THE PRAIRIE STATE

TROY TAYLOR

Globe
Pequot

GUILFORD, CONNECTICUT

Globe
Pequot

An imprint of Globe Pequot, the trade division of The Rowman & Littlefield
Publishing Group, Inc.
4501 Forbes Blvd., Ste. 200
Lanham, MD 20706
www.rowman.com
Distributed by NATIONAL BOOK NETWORK

British Library Cataloguing in Publication Information available

Library of Congress Cataloging-in-Publication Data available

ISBN 978-1-4930-4576-1 (paperback)
ISBN 978-1-4930-4577-8 (e-book)

∞™ The paper used in this publication meets the minimum requirements of
American National Standard for Information Sciences—Permanence of Paper
for Printed Library Materials, ANSI/NISO Z39.48-1992

CONTENTS

INTRODUCTION vii

SOUTHERN ILLINOIS 1
    Ghosts of Cave-in-Rock.. 7
    Horrors of the Old Slave House 9
    The Lonely Spirit of the Devil's Bake Oven.. 14
    The Ghost of Elizabeth Reed.. 16
    The Headless Horseman of Lakey's Creek... 19
    Hauntings of the Original Springs Hotel.. 21

SOUTHWESTERN ILLINOIS... 27
    Lingering Occupants of the Alton Penitentiary 33
    The Infamous McPike Mansion 37
    Strange Phenomena at the First Unitarian Church................................. 39
    Ghosts and Gold at the Old Stone House.. 42
    School Spirit at Lewis and Clark College.. 44
    The Haunted Ruebel Hotel 48
    The Legend of the Hartford Castle... 49
    The Phantom Funeral of Fort de Chartres.. 52

CENTRAL ILLINOIS 57
    The Haunting of the Coliseum Ballroom.. 63
    The Ghost of Mary Hawkins 65
    The Chesterville Witch's Grave 68
    Phantoms of the Lincoln Theater.. 69
    The Cemetery Where the Dead Walk 72
    Abraham Lincoln and the Spiritualists.. 75
    The Ghost Who Wouldn't Leave the Lake Club 78
    The Legends of Voorhies Castle.. 81
    The Tragedy of Towanda Meadows... 86

ILLINOIS RIVER VALLEY 91
    Spirits of Starved Rock... 95
    Haunted Hotel Kaskaskia 97
    The Irritated Ghost of the Ninth Street Pub 98
    The Spring Valley Vampire and the Hatchet Man............ 99

NORTHERN ILLINOIS 103
    Ghosts of the Bartonville Asylum 107
    The House with No Square Corners............................... 111
    Echoes from the Past at Vishnu Springs....................... 112
    Phantom Monks.. 117
    The Watseka Wonder... 118
    The Maple Lake Ghost Light 122
    Elvira of the Woodstock Opera House 125
    The Library Curse and "Old Lady Gray" 126
    The Lingering Spirit of Springdale Cemetery 131

CHICAGO 137
    The St. Valentine's Day Massacre................................. 141
    The Show Did Not Go On... 144
    Ghosts of the Eastland Disaster................................... 148
    Haunted Bachelor's Grove Cemetery............................ 151
    The Italian Bride.. 156
    Jane Addams's Hull House.. 159
    Chicago's Vanishing Hitchhikers 162
    Resurrection Mary.. 166

RECOMMENDED READING 171

ABOUT THE AUTHOR 173

INTRODUCTION

Many have wondered what makes a state like Illinois so haunted. If pressed to pick a single thing most responsible for the ghosts that apparently dwell here, it would be the history of the state itself. Hauntings are believed to be created from violence and bloodshed. And from the beginning, the Prairie State was a place where death thrived and mysteries became commonplace.

The land that became Illinois was once a rolling sea of prairie grass, steeped in legend and lore. It was a rich land, coveted by the settlers and frontiersmen who came west from the American colonies. Its recorded history began with the French explorers in 1673, but humans had already walked here for centuries. The explorers found strange mounds, altars, burial sites, and what appeared to be the ruins of towns and villages. It seemed that a lost civilization had once prospered along the Mississippi River. Who these mysterious dwellers were remains a mystery. They have been called the Mound Builders, thanks to the monuments of earth they left behind, but the people so utterly disappeared that their true identity likely will never be known. They left only silent graves and many unsolved mysteries in their wake.

The French settled in the southwestern regions, along the Mississippi, and in the north, along the soaring bluffs of the Illinois River. They left their own ghostly stories behind after they were replaced by the Americans in the 1700s. This began a time of lawlessness and lack of order in the region. The British overthrew the French occupation and then the British were kicked out of the territory by the new American rule in what were once the eastern colonies. Under the control of the United States, the region was first a part of Virginia, then was included in the Indiana territory, finally becoming the Illinois Territory in 1809. By this time, government had come to the region, and with it came the settlers.

In 1812, war broke out once again with the British, and Illinois became an integral part of the fighting. Along the East Coast and the Canadian border, the American forces fought against the British invasion. Illinois, being the far western frontier, was left out of this part of the war, but the state was torn apart by terrible massacres and battles with the Brits' Indian allies, who created more havoc and committed more horrific murders than the British had ever dreamed.

Shortly after the outbreak of the war, the infamous Fort Dearborn Massacre took place at the site of present-day Chicago. This terrifying incident took the lives of numerous settlers, including many women and children. Other massacres took place along the frontier, leading to the creation of a militia and a number of bloody battles with the Native American population.

After the war, a strong movement began to bring settlers to the region and move the Native Americans out. Not surprisingly, after the hostilities that had taken place during the war, the white men were rarely honest when it came to business dealings with the Indians, and large portions of land were purchased for small amounts of money. In many cases, the Indians were just driven out altogether. Although the last treaty relocating the Indians was not signed until the 1830s, the federal government already controlled most of Illinois by 1818, when it was decided to make the territory into a state.

From the first days of statehood, passion and tragedy ruled Illinois. In the years to come, the prairie created legends like Abraham Lincoln and tangled with the cruelty of slavery. It turned ordinary men like Ulysses S. Grant into heroes and men like Elijah P. Lovejoy into martyrs. Illinois built one of the greatest cities in the nation and sent men to die in the Civil War. The state rioted, burned, became famous for violence and excess, and continued to grow and thrive in more ways than the early settlers ever could have imagined.

This book explores the Prairie State's paranormal side and serves as a guide to its haunted places.

SOUTHERN
ILLINOIS

S outhern Illinois, or "Little Egypt," as it is often called, is a place like no other. Once you leave the central part of Illinois and drive south, it's as though you have entered another state altogether, or perhaps even another world. The region's scenery and landscape become as varied as its inhabitants, with vast acres of forest, caves, swamps, and even the edge of the Ozark Mountains. The people here embody the culture of the region, with strange tales, a rich folklore, and southern drawls that you can rarely find outside of the Deep South.

Below the surface, another place lurks, hidden in the dark forests and forgotten among the bluffs and secret hollows. It's here where the memories of the region's violent history still linger and ghosts and "boogers" dwell. The history of Southern Illinois is as rich, colorful, and turbulent as the landscape. Not surprisingly, the region lends itself to ghost stories and haunts, many of which have become quite well known over the years. Nearly all of them have taken shape from the bloody history of the region.

Where did the nickname Little Egypt come from? The section of Illinois located in the southern tip of the state has long been known as Egypt, and several of the towns here bear names associated with the ancient world: Boaz, Karnak, Carmi, Thebes, Lebanon, Herod, and Cairo, although here it is pronounced "CAY-ROE." Some say this is how the region gained the nickname, but the real roots are thought to be found farther back in Illinois history.

Tradition has it that the people of the prairie region in Central Illinois gave Southern Illinois its nickname when they were forced to travel here for grain after a series of droughts and the terrible winter of 1830, which destroyed their supplies. The settlers in the wagon trains were compared to the ancient Israelites in the Bible, who had to travel to Egypt to buy their grain. The name may have come into use before that, but nevertheless, this anecdote probably helped it become a permanent name.

The region known as Egypt lies just south of a line that extends from the Alton–East St. Louis area to near

Robinson on the eastern side of the state. At this point, the prairie of the north begins to give way to rolling hills that eventually become the foothills of the Ozarks. Agriculture has long been the main industry here, thanks to the mild weather, but rich coal deposits once made it one of the chief mining regions in America.

The first people in Southern Illinois were the ancient Native Americans, who built mysterious mounds and stone forts, but the French were the first white settlers here. They came in the early 1700s and established settlements at Kaskaskia and Prairie du Rocher, along the Mississippi River.

In the early 1800s, American settlers began traveling down the Ohio River to reach the western territories. As they did so, many of them created settlements along the waterway, such as Shawneetown, Golconda, and Elizabethtown. From this land along the river comes one of the bloodiest legends of Southern Illinois.

GHOSTS OF CAVE-IN-ROCK

In the rough and unsettled lands of the western territories, outlaws and pirates soon emerged to prey on the travelers who journeyed down the Ohio River. Many of them established hideouts and settlements along the riverbanks. Perhaps the most famous of these locations was a place called Cave-in-Rock, in the southeastern corner of the state. The cave became the stronghold for pirates who plundered flatboats on the river and murdered and robbed travelers. Around 1800, thieves also began operating a tavern and gambling parlor in the cave, using whiskey, cards, and prostitutes to lure travelers in off the river. Many of these customers found themselves beaten and robbed, and sometimes murdered, after tying up at the crude wharf.

Cave-in-Rock, located close to the town of the same name, was a perfect place for criminal enterprises along the river. At that time, it boasted a partially concealed entrance and a wide view up and down the river. The cave is about a hundred feet deep, with a level floor and a vertical chimney that ascends to the bluff above.

In those early days, many settlers used the Ohio River to begin their travels to the West. It was a simple way to move wagons, people, and goods and eat up huge chunks of the westward trail, but travel by river was anything but serene. The river was filled with hazards like floating logs, known as "sleepers" or "sawyers," that were embedded in the river bottom. If a flatboat hit one of these obstacles, it took hours to repair the damage. River travelers could also encounter unexpected currents, eddies, floods, or even storms that could easily sink a boat.

But these natural hazards were nothing compared with what lurked in the dark corners of Cave-in-Rock. From this vantage point, the pirates could see for many miles up the Ohio River. This unusual formation often called to weary travelers like a beacon, especially when they learned that food, drinks, and rest awaited them inside. In 1800, a man named Wilson brought his family to live in the cave, and he turned it into a dwelling and tavern. He erected a sign along the water's edge that read "Wilson's Liquor Vault & House of Entertainment," and the novelty attracted both river travelers and those who journeyed by land. It soon became a rough spot, famed for its hard cider, whiskey, and women of ill repute.

A band of robbers formed by Wilson became the first pirates to operate on this stretch of the river. They killed whole crews of boats that docked at the cave on their way to New Orleans and stole and sold their cargo. After many months of robberies, the tavern became known from Pittsburgh to New Orleans, and public indignation finally forced the authorities to act. Many of the pirates were arrested, but others were killed or fled the region. Wilson was murdered at the hands of his own men when they learned of the huge reward that had been placed on his head. There is, as they say, no honor among thieves. After Wilson's death, more than sixty bodies of luckless travelers were discovered hidden away in an upper room of the cave.

As years passed, river pirates continued to operate from the cave and eventually came under the leadership of a man named James Ford, a seemingly respectable businessman and ferry boat operator. Ford managed to keep his criminal enterprises secret while he amassed great wealth killing settlers and travelers who came to the river landing near Cave-in-Rock. The pirates stripped and burned wagons and slaughtered travelers and buried them in the woods. No one was ever left alive to identify the outlaws later.

Ford was eventually killed by a vigilante group at the home of a local widow named Simpson. He had gone there for dinner and to provide comfort to the woman, who betrayed him to the vigilantes. He was eating his food at the table, and the woman brought him a candle and asked that he read a letter aloud for her. The candle was a signal, and men waiting outside opened fire, aiming between the logs of the cabin. Ford died with seventeen bullets in his body.

For years after his death, the slaves told stories about how Jim Ford had died and "landed in hell headfirst." At his funeral, attended only by his widow, a few family members and neighbors, and some slaves, a terrible thunderstorm came up. Just as Ford's coffin was being lowered into the ground, lightning flashed and a deafening clap of thunder filled the air, causing one of the slaves to lose his grip on the rope holding the coffin. The box dropped into the grave headfirst and wedged there at a strange angle. The heavy rain that began to fall made it impossible to move the casket, so it was covered over the way that it had fallen. This left Ford to spend eternity standing on his head.

Ford's death did not bring an end to the thievery at Cave-in-Rock, but by the late 1830s, most of the outlaws, pirates, and counterfeiters were driven away, and the bloody past of the place began to fade with time. As years passed, the cave became more of a recreation area than a den of thieves, and it remains a natural attraction in Southern Illinois today.

The legends have never died completely, though, and many still remember the area's blood-soaked past. It's no surprise that travelers on the river often claimed to hear the keening moans of ghosts echoing from the mouth of the cave. This is a place where history has certainly left its mark, proving that in some cases, truth really is stranger than fiction.

HORRORS OF THE OLD SLAVE HOUSE

High on a windswept rise in Southern Illinois is one of the state's most haunted spots. It is called Hickory Hill, and over the years, it has been many things, from plantation house to tourist attraction to chamber of horrors for the men and women once brought here in chains. Thanks to this dark blight on its history, Hickory Hill has long been known by its more familiar name, the Old Slave House. For decades, travelers have come from all over Illinois and beyond to see this mysterious and forbidden place. The secrets of slavery that were hidden here were given up many years ago, but there are other dark whispers about the place. These stories claim that the dead of Hickory Hill do not rest in peace.

Hickory Hill was built by a man named John Hart Crenshaw, a descendant of an old American family with ties to the founding of our country. Crenshaw has a notable spot in the history of Illinois, thanks to both his public and private deeds.

He was born in November 1797, the son of William Crenshaw, in a house on the border of North and South Carolina. His family moved west and settled in New Madrid, Missouri, only to have their home destroyed by the great earthquake of 1811. A short time later, they moved to Saline County, Illinois, and started a farm on the east side of Eagle Mountain. There was a salt well on the farm called Half Moon Lick.

Not long after settling in Illinois, William died and left his eldest son, John, to provide for his mother and six brothers and sisters. By the time he was eighteen, John was already toiling in the crude salt refinery at Half Moon Lick.

Today it is hard to understand the demand that existed for salt in times past. In those days, salt was often used as money or barter material when purchasing goods and supplies. In the early 1800s, a large salt reservation was discovered in Southern Illinois, and the land began to be leased out by the government. Individual operators rented tracts of land and hired laborers, usually poor white and black men, to work them.

In 1829, the government decided to sell off the salt lands to raise money for a new prison and other state improvements in Illinois. The individual operators were given the opportunity to purchase their holdings, and one man who did so was John Hart Crenshaw. He made a number of such purchases over the years and eventually owned several thousand acres of land. At that time, he also owned a sawmill and three salt furnaces for processing.

Eventually, Crenshaw became an important man in Southern Illinois. He had developed wide-reaching business interests that allowed him to amass quite a fortune. In fact, at one point he made so much money that he paid one-seventh of all of the taxes collected in the state. Despite all these accomplishments, Crenshaw is best remembered today for Hickory Hill and his ties to Illinois slavery, kidnapping, and illegal trafficking in slaves—all in a state where slavery was not technically allowed by law. There were exceptions, however, and one exception allowed for slaves to be leased for one-year terms in the salt lands of Gallatin, Hardin, and Saline Counties.

Workers were always needed for the salt mines. The work was backbreaking, hot, and brutal, and it attracted only the most desperate workers. Because of this, slavery became essential to the success of the salt operations.

In fact, it became so essential that salt mine operators like Crenshaw were not averse to kidnapping free blacks and runaway slaves and pressing them into service. They also sold many African Americans into slavery. Night riders of the 1830s and 1840s were always on the lookout for escaped slaves, and they posted men along the Ohio River at night. Runaway slaves were captured and could be ransomed back to their masters or returned for a reward. They also kidnapped free men and their children and sold them in the South. The night riders created a "reverse Underground Railroad," where slaves were spirited away to the southern plantations instead of to the northern cities and freedom.

Local tradition has it that John Hart Crenshaw, who leased slaves to work in the salt mines, kept a number of night riders in his employ to watch for escaped slaves. He used this as a profitable sideline to his legitimate businesses.

Crenshaw was seen as a respected businessman and a pillar of the church and community. No one had any idea that he was holding illegal slaves or that he was suspected of kidnapping black families and selling them into slavery. They would have been even more surprised to learn that the slaves were being held captive in the barred chambers of the third-floor attic of Hickory Hill.

Crenshaw contracted an architect to begin on the house in 1833, but Hickory Hill was not completed until a number of years later. It stands on a high hill, overlooking the Saline River. The structure was built in the Classic Greek style of the time period and is three stories tall. Huge columns, cut from the hearts of individual pine trees, span the front of the house and support wide verandas. On the porch is a main entrance door, and above it, on the upper veranda, is another door that opens onto the balcony. From here, Crenshaw could look out over his vast holdings. He furnished the interior of the house with original artwork and designs that had been imported from Europe. There were thirteen rooms on the first and second floors, each heated with a separate fireplace.

The house was certainly grand, but the most unusual additions to the place were not easily seen. Legend has it that there was once a tunnel that connected the basement to the Saline River, where slaves could be loaded and unloaded at night. In addition, another passageway, large enough to contain a wagon, was built into the rear of the house. It allowed the vehicles to actually enter the house and, according to the stories, let slaves be unloaded where they could not be seen from the outside. The back of the house is still marked by this carriage entrance today.

Located on the third floor of Hickory Hill are the infamous confines of the attic, proof that Crenshaw had something unusual in mind when he contracted the house to be built. The attic can still be reached today by a flight of narrow, well-worn stairs. They exit into a wide hallway, with about a dozen cell-like rooms with barred windows and flat, wooden bunks facing the corridor. Originally the cells were even smaller, and there were more of them, but some were removed in the past. One can only imagine how small and cramped they must have been, because even an average-size visitor to the attic can scarcely turn around in the ones that remain. The corridor between the cells extends from one end of the room to the other. Windows at the ends provided the only ventilation, and during the summer months, the heat in the attic was unbearable. The windows also provided the only source of light. The slaves spent their time secured in these cells, chained to heavy metal rings. Scars remain on the wooden walls and floors today, and chains and heavy balls are still kept on display.

After Crenshaw was indicted for kidnapping a free black woman and her children in 1842, rumors began to spread about his questionable business activities. One of his sawmills was burned down, and over the course of the next few years, his business holdings began to decline. He faced several civil court actions against him, and salt deposits were discovered in both Virginia and Ohio that proved to be more profitable than those in Southern Illinois. To make matters worse for Crenshaw, he was attacked by one of his slaves, resulting in the loss of one leg. The stories maintain that he was beating a woman in his fields one day when an angry slave picked up an ax and severed Crenshaw's leg with it. After that, most of the slaves were sold off, and his operations dwindled with the end of the salt mining.

During the Civil War, Crenshaw sold Hickory Hill and moved to a new farmhouse closer to Equality. He continued farming but also diversified into lumber, railroads, and banks. He died on December 4, 1871, and was buried in Hickory Hill Cemetery, a lonely piece of ground just northeast of his former home.

Whether John Hart Crenshaw rests in peace is unknown, but according to the tales of Little Egypt, many of his former captives most certainly do not. It is said that people have heard mysterious voices in the attic, moaning or singing spirituals. And those accounts are just the beginning.

In 1906, Hickory Hill was purchased by the Sisk family from a descendant of John Hart Crenshaw. It was already a notorious place in the local area, but it soon became even more widely known.

To locals, the house was known more as the Old Slave House than Hickory Hill, thanks to the stories surrounding the place. In the 1920s, the Sisks began to have visitors from outside the area. They would come to the door at just about any hour and request a tour of the place, having heard about it from a local waitress or gas station attendant as they were passing through. The Old Slave House, thanks to a savvy advertising campaign, became a destination point for many travelers and tourists who were so numerous that the owners began charging admission in 1930. For just a dime, or a nickel if you were a child, you could tour the place where "Slavery Existed in Illinois," as the road signs put it.

Shortly after the house became a tourist attraction, visitors began reporting strange phenomena. They complained of odd noises in the attic, especially sounds like cries, whimpers, and the rattling of chains. A number of people told of uncomfortable feelings in the slave quarters, like sensations of intense fear, sadness, and being watched. They also felt cold chills, touches from invisible hands, and unseen figures brushing by them.

The rumored hauntings had little effect on the tourist traffic. If anything, the stories brought more people to the house. Other legends soon began to be attached to Hickory Hill. The most famous is that no one could spend an entire night in the attic. This story got started because of an incident involving a ghost chaser from Benton named Hickman Whittington, who planned to put the ghosts of the house to rest.

Years passed, and despite many attempts, no one managed to spend an entire night in the attic of the Old Slave House. Thrill seekers had a habit of running from the house long before daybreak. Eventually the practice was ended because an overturned lantern started a small fire one night. After that, George Sisk turned down requests for late-night ghost hunting.

He relented on only one occasion. In 1978, Sisk allowed a reporter from Harrisburg named David Rodgers to spend the night in the attic as a Halloween stunt for a local television station. The reporter managed to beat out nearly 150 previous challengers and became the first person in more than a century to spend the night in the slave quarters. Rodgers later admitted that he was queasy going into the house, and he said that his experience in the attic was anything but mundane. He heard many sounds that he could not identify, and he later discovered that his recorder picked up voices that he had not heard.

Visitors and curiosity seekers have continued to tell stories over the years, and the Old Slave House has been a frequent stopping place for ghost hunters, psychic investigators, and supernatural enthusiasts. In 1996, the Old Slave House was closed down because of the declining health of Mr. and Mrs. Sisk. Although it looked as though the house might never reopen, it finally was purchased by the state of Illinois a few years later. Plans are in the works to open the house again in the future as a state historic site. What will become of the ghosts, or at least the ghost stories, is unknown. It seems that legends and lore often don't fare well at official state locations.

Regardless, if you should get the chance, mark Hickory Hill as a historic and haunted place to visit. If you climb those stairs to the attic, you may feel your stomach drop just a little, and you might even be overwhelmed by sadness. Is it your imagination, or does the tragedy of the house still make itself felt here? I can't say for sure, but you will likely find yourself speaking softly in the gloomy, third-floor corridor as your voice lowers in deference to the nameless people who once suffered here.

THE LONELY SPIRIT OF THE DEVIL'S BAKE OVEN

The small town of Grand Tower slumbers peacefully along the muddy banks of the Mississippi River. It was once a booming ironworks town, but little remains of it today. Regardless, Grand Tower has been a Southern Illinois landmark for years, thanks to the legend of the Devil's Bake Oven.

Along the river, this menacing collection of rocks brought death to many travelers. The Native Americans were convinced that evil spirits lurked here, waiting to claim the lives of unwitting victims. The white men who settled the area later acknowledged these beliefs by giving the towering rocks a suitable name. One landmark, a rocky ridge about half a mile long, is called the Devil's Backbone. At the north edge of the Backbone, there is a steep gap and then the Devil's Bake Oven, a larger rock that stands on the edge of the river and rises to nearly 100 feet.

During the steamboat days, the Backbone served as a landmark for river pilots. The two outcroppings of rocks were used as a hiding place for river pirates for years. In 1803, the pirate raids became so bad that a detachment of U.S. cavalrymen was dispatched to drive the outlaws from the area.

The years passed and the town of Grand Tower began to grow. It became a busy river port where goods were shipped and received daily. On the west side of the Devil's Backbone, between the rock formation and the river, is the site of two vanished iron furnaces that operated there until around 1870. Iron ore was brought to these furnaces from Missouri and fired with coal from Murphysboro. It is said that Andrew Carnegie once considered making Grand Tower the "Pittsburgh of the West."

The population soon expanded, and a limekiln was started in Grand Tower, along with a box factory and shipyard. A number of river barges and steamers were constructed here. New businesses came to the area, and even an amusement park was opened on Walker's Hill, just east of town. As time marched on, the city seemed poised to become a major population center, but a cholera epidemic swept through the area and wiped out most of the residents. Within a short time, the coming of the railroads and the decline in river traffic drove away most of the rest. Grand Tower was once a town of more than 4,000 souls, but only a fraction of those still remain. One local even said to me that the graveyards hold more bodies than the town can boast as residents these days.

It was the expansion of the iron industry in Grand Tower that brought about the great legend that still haunts the town today. The Devil's Bake Oven also played a major part in the story; besides serving as a river landmark for years, it became the site of Grand Tower's first ironworks. When the new industry came, several attractive homes were built for the officials of the company, including one built for the superintendent. This house was constructed on top of the Devil's Bake Oven. The foundation of the old house can still be seen on the eastern side of the hill today, and it is here where a lonely ghost is said to walk. It has been reported that her voice is sometimes heard among the ruins of the old house, a once happy place that became one of tragedy and despair.

According to the old story, the ghost is that of the superintendent's young daughter, who was very beautiful but sheltered and naive about life. Her doting father kept her away from the rough men of the foundry, and although she had a number of suitors seeking her hand in marriage, he accepted none of them. Finally, one day, the girl fell in love with one of the young men who came to court her. Her father did not approve and forbade his daughter to see the young man. After she slipped away to meet the young man a few times in the night, her father confined her to the house for a long period of time.

The young man was persuaded to move on from Grand Tower. The girl's father sent some of his largest workers to threaten the man, and money offered by the superintendent sealed the deal. After he departed, the young girl wept over him for days and weeks. At last, because of either grief or some illness brought on by her despair, the young woman died. But apparently she did not leave the Devil's Bake Oven.

The spirit of the young girl is said to have lingered at the site of the house. For many years after her death, visitors to the area reported seeing a strange, mistlike shape that resembled the dead girl walking along the pathway and then vanishing among the rocks near the old house. They often heard moans and wails after her disappearance, and when thunderstorms swept across the region, those moans and wails became bloodcurdling screams.

How long the girl haunted the place, and whether she still does, is unknown. Some believe that her spirit, seeking vengeance for her lost life and love, was the cause of the ruin of Grand Tower. It was after her death that the foundries and businesses failed, an epidemic swept through the region, and the residents of the once thriving town vanished. Legend has it that not long after the girl's death, her guilt-ridden father committed suicide, unable to cope with what he had done. When the foundry closed down soon after, his once fine home was razed, and its timbers were used to build a railway station. Only its stone foundations remain.

Does the ghost still haunt the Devil's Bake Oven today? If she does, she probably finds the area unfamiliar to her now. The stone landmarks are still there, but the land around them is greatly changed. The town of Grand Tower has faded into a scattering of houses, and there is little to remind us of the rich history of this small area.

And little to remind us of the young girl who once died here of a broken heart and whose spirit refuses to rest in peace.

THE GHOST OF ELIZABETH REED

There likely are incidents in the history of any region that the residents would just as soon forget. Among these incidents were the public hangings of yesterday—and when tragedy was mixed in with the death, the stories and impressions left behind from such incidents did not quickly fade away. On May 23, 1845, Elizabeth "Betsy" Reed earned an infamous place in Illinois history as the first, and last, woman hanged in the state, in a grove of trees at the edge of what is now Lawrenceville.

The story of the strange events surrounding Betsy's death began in the summer of 1844, in a place called Purgatory Swamp. This was a rural, backwoods area at the time that Betsy and her husband, Leonard, lived there. They resided in a log cabin about eight miles south of Palestine and half a mile north of Heathsville. The old cabin has been gone for many years, and Purgatory Swamp is long forgotten, but in 1844, nearly everyone in Illinois knew just where it was.

During the hot days of that summer, Leonard Reed became ill. A neighbor girl, Eveline Deal, was called to the cabin to help care for him. She later testified that she was present when a doctor came to call on the sick man. After a brief examination, the doctor announced that Leonard was too sick to survive. After the doctor had left the cabin, Eveline claimed that she saw Betsy pour some sort of white powder into her husband's sassafras tea. Betsy told the young girl that it was medicine. Before the doctor returned the following day, August 15, Leonard Reed was dead.

At the time of the funeral, Betsy seemed to be a grieving widow. It was not until later that her behavior became suspect—perhaps it was after Eveline Deal mentioned the "medicine" that Reed had slipped into the dead man's tea. Suspicion soon fell on Betsy, and rumors began to spread that someone should look into Leonard's death. It might not have been a simple fever that killed him, after all.

At that time, Elizabeth Reed was thought of as a strange woman with a "very peculiar and hardened disposition." Her strange behavior, even before her husband's death, led many people to think of her as a witch, and there is no doubt that she made an interesting spectacle on occasions when she came into town. She is believed to have had some sort of facial disfigurement and always wore a white cap or white band over her head, attached to which was a veil. She constantly wore the veil, hiding her features and setting local tongues to wagging. It was no surprise that Betsy was accused of murdering her husband, and even less of a surprise that most people believed that she committed the crime.

Whispers, rumors, and speculation swirled around the area, and eventually the Crawford County sheriff was forced into launching an investigation. There was little to suggest that Betsy had actually committed any crime, save for the account from Eveline Deal, so the investigation was started more to settle the unrest in the community than because any evidence existed of wrongdoing. As it turned out, though, the investigation would make it apparent that Betsy was deeply involved in her husband's death.

A search of the Reed cabin turned up a piece of brown paper that matched the description of the paper from which Eveline had seen Betsy pouring her husband's "medicine." Sheriff Thorn was able to trace the paper to a druggist in Russellville, who admitted that it was the same type of paper he used to dispense various types of medicine. In addition, it was also the same type of paper in which he had wrapped a quantity of arsenic for Elizabeth Reed! To make matters worse for Betsy, several witnesses verified that they had seen her in Russellville while she was making her purchase from the druggist.

Although such scant evidence would not be enough to convict anyone of murder today, in those times it was enough to get Betsy arrested and charged with her husband's murder. She was placed in the county jail in Palestine in August 1844, and shortly after her incarceration, the wooden jail mysteriously burned to the ground. This further fueled the speculation that she was a witch, especially since there seemed to be no cause for the blaze. Betsy was moved to a loft above the sheriff's home and fastened with a chain to a sturdy bed. She remained there for several weeks while preparation was made for her trial.

A grand jury found the evidence to be enough to charge her for murder in September, and a change of venue was requested and approved. Betsy was then transported to Lawrenceville in Lawrence County for her trial, which was finally held in April 1845.

The trial lasted for only a few days and ended with Elizabeth Reed being found guilty of murder. She was sentenced to hang on May 23 and returned to the jail to await her execution day.

People from all over the state as well as from Indiana came to Lawrence County to witness the death sentence being carried out. By some estimates, crowds of curiosity seekers swelled to nearly 20,000 people. Betsy left the jail and rode to the site of her hanging while sitting on her own coffin in the back of a wagon. A friend who had been giving her religious instruction in jail was at her side. Betsy had been baptized after her conviction and had found the Lord in jail. She came to her execution dressed in a long, white robe, and as the wagon approached the site where the execution was to be carried out, onlookers were startled to hear her praying loudly and singing religious hymns at the top of her lungs.

Betsy was led onto the gallows and stood as her funeral sermon was given by the Reverend John Sneed. She loudly commented on everything the preacher said, and her enthusiastic responses were the only sound that was heard at the scene. The mob of people stood by watching in absolute silence.

When the sermon ended, Betsy stepped bravely onto the trapdoor, and a black hood was placed over head, followed by a noose. Sheriff Thorn had tried in vain to find someone else to hold the rope that would send the woman into the afterlife, and he finally was forced to do the honors himself. Just after noon, he cut the rope and the trap dropped under her feet. When Betsy plunged down through the opening, her body spun around several times, but she put up very little struggle. When she was dead, her body was taken down and placed in a shallow grave directly beneath the gallows. It did not remain there for long, though. Relatives soon dug up the remains and placed them next to her husband in Baker Cemetery, just outside Heathsville.

Those who visit the small graveyard today can find the graves of Elizabeth and Leonard Reed under an unobtrusive marker in the southwest corner of the grounds. The stone is a simple one, bearing the names of both. Below Leonard's name are the words "killed by murder," and beneath Elizabeth's is the inscription "killed by hanging." Even the most jaded visitor to the cemetery admits to feeling a little unsettled to read these peculiar memorials written so plainly, side by side.

It's no surprise that over the years, locals have reported hearing the sounds of a woman weeping coming from this small, darkened graveyard and seeing the apparition of a lady in white flitting among the stones. It seems that even after all these years, Betsy's spirit does not rest in peace.

THE HEADLESS HORSEMAN OF LAKEY'S CREEK

Located in Southern Illinois is the small town of McLeansboro, where for nearly 150 years, a headless rider has been seen haunting a concrete bridge that spans the murky waters of Lakey's Creek. Though the identity of this spectral rider has long been known in the area, only a few people are aware of why this phantom still rides.

The creek that is spanned by the bridge was named after an early settler in this community. After Lakey arrived here, he began building a small cabin near the creek, just off a main road that connected Mount Vernon to Carmi. Lakey made quick work of the cabin, although he often could be found stopping his work and chatting with travelers and neighbors who passed by. This was what he reportedly was doing on the last evening that he was seen alive. A few neighbors later recalled riding by and stopping to talk with Lakey, who had completed the walls of his home and was now cutting clapboards for the roof.

The next morning, a neighbor from the settlement stopped to drop off some extra eggs for Lakey. He called out to Lakey, but receiving no answer, he looked around the back of the house and found a gruesome sight. He discovered Lakey's bloody and headless body beside a tree stump. His head had rolled a few feet away and now lay propped against the murder weapon—Lakey's own ax!

The news of the horror quickly spread, and settlers came to examine the scene. The local sheriff was dispatched, but he was as befuddled as everyone else. Lakey had been a friendly man, with no known enemies and no hidden wealth to speak of, and there was nothing to suggest that he had struggled with anyone. The killer, whoever it might have been, was never found. Lakey was buried next to his unfinished cabin, but it seems that he did not stay in his grave for long.

One night, a short time after Lakey's funeral, two men who lived on the west side of McLeansboro were walking near the cabin. Suddenly they spotted a headless figure on a large, black horse. The specter appeared alongside the creek and followed along with them as they walked. Neither of the men spoke, as they were too afraid to say anything, and the rider was also silent. As the men headed down into the shallow crossing of the stream, the rider turned as well. The men waded out into the middle of the creek, and as they did, the horseman turned left, passed downstream, and then inexplicably vanished into a deep pool near the river crossing.

The two men hurried home, and though they hesitated to tell anyone what they had seen, they soon found that it didn't matter. Other locals also began seeing the rider. Two nights later, a small group of travelers from the western side of the state spotted the rider and told others about it. The horseman began to be seen on a regular basis, giving birth to an eerie legend. Locals believed the ghost was that of Lakey himself, searching for the man who killed him. They said that his ghost followed the travelers until he could be sure that they were not the man he was looking for.

The rider continued to join travelers as they crossed the river, but he would always turn and vanish. As time passed, the river crossing was replaced with a bridge, and the stories changed to say that the rider now appeared on the riverbank, would cross the bridge to the center of the river, and then vanish.

Many years have passed since then, and the legend of Lakey's ghost is largely forgotten. Perhaps the pace of modern life has rendered the ghost and his phantom steed somewhat obsolete. Although it is seldom told, the story hasn't been completely lost, leading some to speculate that perhaps Lakey is still out there. Perhaps he still seeks the justice, or the vengeance, that he never found. Do travelers still encounter the ghost as they cross the old bridge over Lakey's Creek? Perhaps not in the way that they used to, but many area residents will assure you that both Lakey and his legend live on. Some still say that it is not uncommon for people walking near the bridge to hear odd sounds coming from the roadway. They claim that these sounds are the clip-clop of a horse's hooves on the pavement, but that the horse that walks there is never seen. Could it be Lakey out on a midnight ride?

HAUNTINGS OF THE ORIGINAL SPRINGS HOTEL

Just off the downstate Illinois highways, tucked away in the shadows of the cornfields, is the small town of Okawville. Though it is quiet today, it was once one of the busiest towns in Southern Illinois, as people from across the country came to take in the waters of the mineral springs that still exist beneath the town. At one time, there were dozens of resorts offering healing baths, but only one remains.

The Original Springs Hotel rests on North Hanover Street in Okawville and today is the only continually operating mineral spring in the state of Illinois. It is a place of history and mystery that still draws people from the surrounding area and beyond. They come here hoping to experience not only the rejuvenating waters of the old spring, but also the strange and ghostly atmosphere of the place.

The mysterious waters of Okawville were first discovered in 1867. Rudolph Plegge was the owner of a harness and saddle shop and, looking for a source of water for his business, began digging his own well. He didn't notice anything odd about the water until it began eating through his copper and tin kettles. Curious, a local medical man decided to test the water and discovered that it had a high mineral content. When the doctor heard this, he made arrangements to have one of his rheumatic patients who was not responding to any other treatments come bathe in the water. The man was almost immediately cured.

Although Plegge soon began dreaming of building a hotel and bathhouse in Okawville, those dreams were not realized until years later. In 1884, the wife of the Reverend J. F. Schierbaum of Edwardsville came to Okawville to take in the waters. At that time, she was said to have been a hopeless invalid and had visited all of the best doctors in St. Louis, who offered her no relief from her pains and ailments. She came to Okawville, bathed in the water, and was restored to perfect health. She was so overjoyed that she persuaded her husband and several other ministers in the German Evangelical Church to buy Plegge's business and construct a hotel on the site.

By September of that year, plans were made to build the hotel. It was to be a grand structure made of brick that would hold dining rooms, a large kitchen, and forty-six rooms. Work was started right away, and the business that followed caused the place to be expanded several times in the coming years.

As the years passed, the town of Okawville and the hotel both prospered. The hotel changed owners a few times, and then in 1892, it burned to the ground. It was soon rebuilt and expanded, and by 1898, the owners were bottling the water and shipping it all over the state, bringing more fame to the Original Springs Hotel. Around 1900, the hotel was sold back to the Reverend Schierbaum. After his death in 1904, his family continued to run the place, making changes and expanding the operations through the early 1900s. Business remained brisk through 1911, when Anna Schierbaum, the Reverend's wife, died after a lengthy illness. She had been managing the hotel since her husband's death, and it fell to her son Ben, who had been a clerk for several years, to take over.

The following year, Ben married Alma Schulze, the daughter of C. L. Schulze, who operated a store in the brick building across the street from the hotel. Their marriage apparently was a rocky one, and though no details of their troubles have been found, Alma left Ben in November 1916, not long after the hotel closed for the winter season. Not having any idea where she had gone, he spent several days searching for her. He soon returned home, depressed, and late one evening went to see her parents at their store across the street. They were unable or unwilling to help the young man, and he returned to the empty hotel.

Five days later, a traveling salesman, who had been looking for another hotel in town and was directed to the Original Springs by mistake, walked into the lobby of the place. Even though the hotel had been closed for the season, he found the front door unlocked and called out to see if anyone was around. The front desk was deserted, so he started down the main hallway, past the desk and hotel office. After walking a short distance, he noticed a corridor that turned off the left, which was then a passageway that led out to the bathhouse. He took only a few steps when he saw the huge pool of dried blood on the floor. Startled, he looked to see a man, later identified as Ben Schierbaum, slumped against the wall. Blood was sprayed all over the hallway, and a good portion of his head was missing. In his lap was a double-barreled shotgun, and next to it was a curtain rod that had been used to pull the trigger. Several letters and his wife's photograph were lying on the floor. Nearby, out of reach of the blood, was a letter that had been written to his father-in-law, Mr. Schulze, asking him to call the coroner and his brother Dan, and then to "forget the whole matter." Ben had taken his own life in despair over losing his beloved Alma.

The hotel was sold off in 1919 and began a period of decline that resulted in the hotel becoming a hangout for Southern Illinois gangsters during the 1920s. The Great Depression caused hardship all over America, but it actually revived Okawville and the hotel. Radio ads brought in large crowds from St. Louis and the surrounding area. The hotel was constantly filled during the early 1930s but started to slack off by 1933. Business eventually became so bad that the owner, Conrad Paeben, committed suicide by poisoning himself. The management of the hotel was taken over by two of its employees, Tom Rogers and Louis Elardin. With the help of a local banker, they were able to keep the hotel open.

The hotel continued to draw weekend visitors, even during the difficult days of World War II, but it was far from the capacity crowds of the hotel's heyday. Owner Tom Rogers became known for being increasingly stranger and more eccentric. He seemed to be content with the few bathers who came each year and gave up on trying to promote the hotel. He took to wandering the empty corridors of the hotel each night, until one morning in March 1962, he was discovered lying dead in one of the upstairs rooms. A search for heirs was started, but none were ever found. His estate was settled in October of that year, and the hotel was sold to Albert and Doris Krohne.

When the Krohnes took over the place, it had not been changed or updated in years. The only modern convenience in the rooms was a single lightbulb that hung from a cord in the center of each room's ceiling. Communal bathrooms were located on each floor. With funds available for renovations, the Krohnes went to work. Some of the rooms were equipped with sinks and toilets, although usually just by partitioning off a section of the room, but others were equipped with showers. For several years, there were three categories of rooms to let at the hotel: good, better, and best. The good rooms had no facilities, the better rooms had sinks and toilets, and the best rooms had showers. Tubs were later added to the deluxe rooms, which were priced accordingly.

In early 1965, the Boiler Room Lounge and Restaurant was opened to the general public. Before this, the kitchen had been available only to hotel guests. Now there were dances and live music on the weekends, and it became quite a popular place. In 1972, excavations were started for a swimming pool. For some time, it was an outdoor pool that was used only during the summer months, but it is now enclosed and kept nicely heated all year round.

The last change in ownership for the Original Springs occurred in May 1990, when the Krohnes sold out to the present owners, Don and Mary Rennegarbe, who continue working to restore the hotel to its former glory. The Original Springs has weathered fires, the Great Depression, suicides, changes in management, two world wars, and the changing tastes of the American people. Through it all, the hotel has continued to stand as a monument to the past. Even today, people come here from all over the region to take in the healing Okawville waters and soak up some of the ambience of days gone by.

But healing waters and good food are not the only things that people come here for. Some come looking for ghosts. And thanks to the unusual history of the hotel and the colorful parade of characters that passed through it, ghosts apparently are something that many of them find.

Don and Mary Rennegarbe heard rumors and stories of unexplainable phenomena almost as soon as they took over the aging hotel. Staff members and desk clerks started to tell of strange noises that they heard in the building at night, including pacing footsteps in otherwise empty hallways. Figures were sometimes seen out of the corner of the eye, doors opened and closed by themselves, the tinkling sound of old-time music echoed in the corridors, and as one of the employees recently told me, some had the constant feeling that someone was watching them.

Not long after taking over the hotel, Mary set up her office in the part of the hotel that was just behind the swimming pool. The office was on the second level, and a balcony stretched across the front, just above the pool. It was on this balcony that guests and employees alike began to report sightings of a spectral woman in a white dress. She was described as wearing a long dress with a high waist and a hat that was in the fashion of the early years of the 1900s. No matter how she was seen, though, her face was always shadowed by the hat and remained unrecognizable. The sightings near this part of the hotel continued for several years, but then ceased at about the same time that Mary moved her office to a room just off the lobby.

Within a short time of moving into her new office, Mary had a strange experience while working late in the hotel one night. She had just closed the restaurant and was sitting behind the desk with the clerk who was on duty. They were quietly talking when they heard a door open in the main corridor. Glancing out, they saw a man in bedclothes come out of the room that was just down the hall from Mary's office. The man stepped out into the hallway and looked around in bewilderment. Finally, with a puzzled look on his face, he walked up to the desk and asked Mary and the clerk a strange question for so late at night: Had they seen a woman in the hallway?

They told him that they hadn't and asked him what was wrong. The man explained that he had been lying in bed with his wife when he began to have the uncomfortable feeling that someone was watching him. He finally sat up and looked around the shadowed room to see a woman standing near the end of the bed. She was wearing a long, white dress and had a large hat on that hid part of her face. She stood there for a moment, looking at him, then turned and walked toward the door. She never hesitated before passing right through it! The man refused to believe his eyes, and he ran to the door and looked out into the corridor, expecting to see a flesh-and-blood person walking down the hall—but it was empty.

Since that time, the woman in white has been seen again in this same room and has also been spotted in the hallway outside the room. She has been seen in other places too. One afternoon, a food delivery driver came into the restaurant while Mary was working. He was a regular driver on the route and came to the Original Springs, traveling between St. Louis and Indiana, on a weekly basis. He saw a woman looking out the window on an upper floor and asked Mary who she was. Mary told him no one was up there that day, but he insisted that he had seen a woman in a white dress and hat looking out at him. Mary asked him where he had seen her, and he took her outside and pointed to three windows on the north side of the bathhouse. The woman, he said, had been looking out the one in the middle. Even though no woman would be in that part of the hotel, as it's the men's bathhouse, Mary checked the room. She found that it was not only empty, but locked.

The strange incidents and eerie sightings continue to this day. Many of the staff members at the hotel refuse to go upstairs and into the older wing at night. They have often heard strange noises in some of the locked rooms, as well as footsteps in the hallways. One particularly unsettling room is a large suite that was converted from three smaller rooms—one of which was where former owner Tom Rogers was found dead back in March 1962.

Who haunts the Original Springs Hotel? Could the sounds and apparitions be spirits from the glory days of the hotel, who refuse to cross over to the other side? Might Ben Schierbaum, Tom Rogers, or other characters from the building's history be lingering still? And who is the mysterious woman in white who has been seen on numerous occasions? Perhaps she is Alma Schierbaum, Ben's wife, still haunting the hotel where her husband met his tragic end, trapped by guilt over having been the reason for his death.

SOUTHWESTERN
ILLINOIS

The French were the first to settle along the lands of Southwestern Illinois. From the borders of what is now Randolph County to as far north as Alton, French settlements sprang up and prospered for many years.

After the War of 1812, the region became a prime area for settlement. The early settlers came mostly from areas to the east and south, such as Kentucky and Indiana. They quickly found that the frontier was not without its dangers, and many did not survive. The lands along the Mississippi River were inhospitable and dangerous. No roads existed, and thick timber and wild rivers and creeks restricted just about any sort of movement by land. Most newcomers to the Illinois country used the rivers to navigate, in spite of the many dangers involved. As they made their way up the Mississippi to where the rivers converged, they traveled along, camped on, and eventually settled at one of the most fertile areas of Illinois, the American Bottoms.

This stretch of the Mississippi River floodplain is where the early Native Americans made their homes and built the great mounds of centuries past. The French flourished here before being joined by British colonists and Americans. The population of what was called the American Bottoms was concentrated in settlements such as Kaskaskia, Cahokia, and Prairie du Rocher in the early years. Native Americans also roamed the region, as it was plentiful with game, but they were later driven out after hostilities during the war. The American Bottoms was a place of great beauty but also of great mystery and strange happenings.

Much of the danger that plagued the daily lives of those who resided in the American Bottoms came from the Native American populace, but they also faced threats from weather and disease. Humidity and heat always seemed to settle along the river and the land was often flooded, leaving water that was slow to drain. Ponds and lakes frequently formed in areas where drainage was poor, and small streams clogged with leaves after storms and created problems for homes and fields. In the wet places and swampy spots, swarms of mosquitoes thrived, although no one recognized what a health problem they were for many years.

The American Bottoms was believed to be an unhealthy area. A strange form of malaria was common, but doctors had no idea what caused it, and it was referred to as simply a fever or ague. They believed the illness was caused by a noxious gas that came from the swamps and from wet and rotting vegetation. With no quinine available, sufferers were forced to allow the fever to run its course. The attacks started with a series of cold chills, which left the victims shaking, their teeth chattering. This was followed by flushes of burning heat and terrible pains in the head and back. Those with the sickness were left to simply "sweat it out," although the fevers often recurred.

Another problem with the spread of disease was the lack of personal cleanliness common on the frontier. In the heat of summer, flies plagued the cabins, which had no screens on the doors or windows. Little soap was available, and what was on hand was rarely used. The settlers were also ignorant of sanitation practices, and human and animal waste often contaminated the drinking supply. With the lack of hygiene, childhood diseases—typhoid, tuberculosis, dysentery, and smallpox—ran rampant among the pioneers.

Life on the frontier was never easy, and the death and tragedy that sometimes triumphed over the hard lives of the settlers gave birth to legends, superstitions, and ghost stories. This is an old and strange region—and one of the most haunted in the state.

LINGERING OCCUPANTS OF THE ALTON PENITENTIARY

I do not believe there is any other Illinois town along the Mississippi River that is as haunted as Alton. Mark Twain once called the place a "dismal little river town," but it has since earned a more distinguished reputation as one of the most haunted small towns in America. The history of the place is filled with all of the makings of ghosts and ghost stories—death, murder, disease, tragedy, the Civil War, the Underground Railroad, and much more. At no other spot in this small town has the history left a blacker mark than at the site of the first prison in Illinois.

Construction on the first penitentiary in the state was completed in Alton in 1833. Conditions were grim almost from the beginning, and the prison became known as a horrific place, plagued by rats, vermin, and disease. There was always a lack of clean clothing, fresh water, edible food, and medical care, and according to records, many of the men who served time there died within a few months of their release, their health broken.

By the 1850s, the situation was so bad that Dorothea Dix, a social reformer and leader in the movement to improve conditions for prisoners and the mentally ill, led a crusade to stop the Alton prison from being used. Her reports about the place led to a heated controversy that eventually ended in a legislative investigation and the construction of a new prison near Joliet, which was completed in 1859. Prisoners from Alton were soon transferred there, and by 1860, the Alton Penitentiary was abandoned.

In the early years of the Civil War, Alton became a military post, thanks to its location on the Missouri border and its access to the river. By 1862, it had become apparent that the war was not going to come to a swift end, and more space was needed for the growing numbers of Confederate prisoners of war. Permission was granted to Union commanders to take over the empty Alton Penitentiary for use as a military prison. Within three days of the arrival of the first prisoners, the penitentiary was already overcrowded. The maximum capacity of the institution was estimated at 800, but throughout most of the war, it held between 1,000 and 1,500 prisoners and often more—sometimes as many as 5,000.

Most of the prisoners remained in their cells or had limited access to the yard, where the drinking water and latrines could be found. The prison had no water supply. A well was located on the grounds, but soon after the prisoners of war were transferred, the water was found to be contaminated. The situation was remedied by hauling huge water kegs from the river, using a six-mule team wagon. The drinking water was stored in a trench located just a short distance away from a similar container used as the latrine. Heat was supplied to the prison by wood-burning stoves set up in the corridors.

As the war continued, new prisoners arrived in Alton on a regular basis. Living conditions in the prison were unbearable. Most of the men were poorly clothed, food was often withheld as a punishment or was not edible when it was given, bathing facilities were not available, and gnats and lice were common, as were rats and other vermin. The prevailing diseases at the Alton prison included malaria, pneumonia, dysentery, scurvy, and anemia, and they felled more men than gunshots ever could. Then, in 1863, several isolated cases of smallpox broke out among the prisoners. Weakened by poor diets and filthy living conditions, the men were helpless against the disease, which began to spread and quickly turned into an epidemic.

At the time of the outbreak, the prison population numbered almost 2,000 in quarters that were designed for many less. The men slept three in a bed, ate standing up, and used a common latrine. Nothing was clean in the prison, and the men were often unshaved and filthy. Their sleeping mattresses were never changed or washed, and the prison yard was filled with pools of stagnant water and urine.

The smallpox virus could live for hours on contaminated clothing and blankets and had an incubation period of two weeks. It was spread to others long before the carrier ever realized he was sick. And little could be done for those with the disease, other than to let it run its course. Smallpox victims became completely dehydrated, and as the disease progressed, they developed oozing pustules on their legs, arms, and faces. Survivors were often badly scarred.

By the second month, prison guards were also coming down with smallpox. More and more men became sick, and both prisoners and guards began to die. It was said that those soldiers who were not sick had to be threatened with court-martial to get them to continue with their duties. The disease also spread into the city of Alton, killing many residents. In the early days of the epidemic, as the prison death toll first began to climb, Alton's mayor, Edward T. Drummond, refused to have any of the prisoners treated away from the prison. There were no hospitals in the city of Alton in those days. The patients were quartered in hallways, storage rooms, and stables, as the prison hospital had only five beds. Before the outbreak, there had been about half a dozen deaths per week in the prison, but soon there were more than five a day.

The sick and dying men were overflowing from the converted hospitals and sick rooms, and the situation became dire over what to do with the bodies of the dead. The prison "dead house" was simply a shed in the yard where bodies were kept until they could be buried. This soon became woefully inadequate for the needs of the prison. The people of Alton began to panic and demanded that the sick and dead be taken somewhere outside the city limits. The failing men and those who succumbed to the illness were taken to a small island on the Mississippi called Sunflower Island. Located on one end of the island was a dilapidated summer cottage, which was commandeered and turned into a hospital pesthouse, a ward to quarantine those with deadly diseases. It too became quickly overcrowded. A number of healthy prisoners were ordered to act as hospital attendants and stretcher bearers, although few of them were well enough to work. Prisoners, guards, and doctors feared going to the island, afraid they would never return. Prisoners and guards also transported wrapped bodies to the island, placing them in trenches that had been dug.

The smallpox epidemic continued to rage at the prison throughout the winter of 1863 and into the following spring. In the summer of 1864, a group of St. Louis nuns from the Daughters of Charity arrived at the prison. They demanded better medical supplies, an actual hospital building, and permission to conduct burial services for the men. A new hospital was authorized on the grounds, and construction was completed by that autumn. By the end of the summer, new cases of smallpox were no longer reported, and the pesthouse on Sunflower Island was closed down. Those who were buried there remain unknown today, and their graves, as well as the island itself, have vanished.

Shortly after the war, the locations of the island graves were lost, thanks to flooding along the Mississippi River. The island was shunned by the residents, some believed, because of the chance that traces of smallpox might linger there. Others believed that it was avoided for another reason altogether—because the ghosts of the men buried in unmarked graves still roamed the island.

The Alton Penitentiary was closed down after the war and abandoned, despite a brief effort to have it used as a state facility once again. The walls around the prison yard were torn down between 1870 and 1875, and most of the stone was hauled off for road construction projects. The area where the prison yard was located was turned into a public park.

Some of the walls of the old prison continued to stand for years, but by the 1940s, only scattered ruins were left. The last section was finally moved in 1973 and reconstructed nearby as a monument to the past. The area where the prison was located is now a public parking lot. Today only this small portion of the wall still remains on the site of the penitentiary, where visitors can find historical information and displays about the prison and the Civil War.

As the years have passed, the old Alton Penitentiary has become the source of a number of ghostly legends around the area. For years, the historic site and the surrounding area have been the scene of ghostly reports. Many of the tales date back even farther than recent times.

In the days after the war, the old prison building remained on the back of the lot, slowly crumbling into ruin. As one might imagine, the temptation of the old prison often proved too much for visitors to resist, and many of them explored the empty corridors, abandoned cells, and deserted staircases. But these visitors soon found that the old prison apparently was not as empty as they had believed. Soon tales began to filter out of the area about ghostly voices, strange sounds, screams and cries, and eerie weeping and moaning that came from places where no one living could be found. The disturbing tales continued for decades, even up until the time that the remnants of the prison were finally demolished.

People also spoke of seeing the spectral images of former prisoners still wandering about on the property. These figures had the chilling habit of vanishing without a trace when approached or confronted. They would be there one moment and gone the next, and turning the old prison yard into a parking lot seemed to have little effect on them.

Even in recent years, passersby have claimed to see apparitions of men and soldiers still lingering on these grounds, usually describing them as being very ragged. The ghosts appear and then vanish with no warning. Could they be the lost souls of soldiers who suffered and died here, a result of the horror and tragedy that occurred in the prison during some of America's darkest days?

THE INFAMOUS MCPIKE MANSION

When just about any native of the Alton area thinks of a haunted house, normally one name comes to mind—the infamous McPike Mansion on Alby Street. Simply based on the number of stories that have swirled about the place, it's obvious that the McPike Mansion is the most haunted house in Alton.

The house was built in 1869 for Henry Guest McPike. The McPike family can be traced back to Scotland, and Henry McPike's ancestry includes a number of patriots who fought during the Revolutionary War, including Captain Mose Guest McPike of New Jersey and Captain James McPike, both of whom were at Valley Forge with George Washington.

James McPike headed west to Kentucky in 1795, bringing with him his sons, John and Richard. Henry McPike was a son of John McPike and came to Alton as a very young man in 1847. Henry soon became active in the business and political community of Alton. Over a period of years, he was involved in a number of different companies, working as a real estate agent, box manufacturer, and insurance executive, among other things. He also became the president of the oldest horticultural society in Illinois.

His political aspirations did not get off to a quick start, although he did have an interest in the abolitionist movement. His father had been the editor of a Whig newspaper (the Whig party later became the Republicans in the time of Abraham Lincoln) and was an early advocate of the abolition of slavery. Despite this, Henry McPike never sought political office, although it was offered to him many times.

During the Civil War, McPike was called upon to act as deputy provost marshal of the district, and this placed him in a management position in the War Department. After this, he was said to have begun acting as a representative in many conventions and with the City Council. This eventually led to a stint as the mayor of Alton from 1887 to 1891.

The McPike Mansion was constructed in an Italianate-Victorian style and stands as one of the more elaborate homes in Alton. It contains sixteen rooms and a vaulted wine cellar and was originally built on a country estate of fifteen acres that Henry called Mount Lookout. Thanks to his interest in all things horticultural, the estate was planted with rare trees and shrubs, orchards, flowers, and extensive vineyards. Henry also was the propagator of the McPike grape, which became known across the country.

There is no question that this was one of the most beautiful homes in the area. The McPike family lived at the estate for some time after Henry's death, but records are unclear about the dates. Some say they stayed in the house until around 1936, but other records show that Paul A. Laichinger purchased it in 1908 and either lived in the house or rented it out to tenants until his death around 1930.

The years have not been kind to the McPike Mansion, and it has been abandoned and in disrepair since the 1950s. During that time, weather and vandals have caused some pretty major damage to the structure. The house once had a number of marble fireplaces and some very extravagant woodwork, but all of that was stolen while it was unoccupied. Windows are broken, the plaster is cracked and destroyed, floors have deteriorated to the point they are not safe to walk on, and worse. The place is in desperate need of repair, but the enormous price tag makes this a daunting task.

But some hope does remain that the McPike Mansion will not become just a memory. In 1994, Sharyn and George Luedke purchased the house at auction, and they have been working for more than a decade to restore the home to its former glory.

Beyond just being entranced with the history of the house, Sharyn believes the mansion is haunted. Her unusual encounters at the house carry much more weight, given the time she has spent there, than the claims of trespassers, so-called psychics, and curiosity seekers who come to the house simply because it looks haunted. Hundreds of stories have circulated about the mansion, from the chilling to the downright silly, but Sharyn's claims that the ghost of Paul Laichinger haunts the place seem to be the most credible. He is one of the few spirits alleged to haunt the place for whom a real historical connection exists.

Sharyn says that she had her first encounter with Paul's ghost about six weeks after she bought the house. She was on the property watering some plants and saw a man standing in the window, looking out toward her in the front yard. A chill came over her, but she noted that the man, who vanished, was wearing a striped shirt and a tie. Sharyn has a photograph of Paul Laichinger wearing an identical outfit.

Another spirit in the house is thought to be a domestic servant that Sharyn calls Sarah. She was little more than a presence with an assumed name until a man came by the house one day and presented the Luedkes with some books that he had removed from the house seventeen years before. One of the books had the name Sarah Wells written inside of it. Since that time, Sharyn has been hugged by this spirit, and she and her husband have occasionally caught the scent of lilac on the third floor.

While I'm not convinced that all the local stories are true, there does seem to be more there than meets the eye. I have visited the house many times and one evening witnessed some unusual phenomena. A group of us were gathered in the wine cellar, which is below the basement, and one woman became uncomfortable in the small, enclosed space and asked to go upstairs. Another woman accompanied her upstairs, and the rest of us waited patiently for her to return. After a few moments, the sound of the second woman's footsteps could be heard descending the steps and the basement stairs and crossing the basement floor. A short pause followed, and then the metal door to the wine cellar opened, scraping across the stone floor—but there was no one there! Both of the women were still upstairs, and no one else had come down the steps—no one human, that is.

STRANGE PHENOMENA AT THE FIRST UNITARIAN CHURCH

The first Unitarian Society was started in Alton in 1836. The Unitarian faith was considered the bastion of the free thinkers in its early years, but it attracted many writers and poets of the time, such as Ralph Waldo Emerson and Henry David Thoreau. It is based on the freedom of belief among its members, never stressing an official creed but allowing individuals to hold their own particular beliefs. The Alton group grew and flourished during the nineteenth century and constructed its first church building in the 1850s. A disastrous fire destroyed the original church, but a new building was constructed in 1905 and remains on Third Street in Alton today.

A number of men served the church as pastors over the years, but one of them left a greater mark on the church than any of the others. His name was Phillip Mercer, and not only did he gain a reputation as a kind and caring man, but he also left a lasting impression on the church because, according to some, Phillip Mercer has never left.

The Reverend Phillip Mercer was born and raised in England and came to America when he was just eighteen years old. No one ever really knew him well, and he always had a rather strict sense of propriety, never revealing much about his personal life. Everyone he met liked him very much, however, and he was always described as a friendly and caring man, although a bit of worrier when it came to his health.

Mercer lived in St. Louis for a time and often spoke of the great amount of reading that he had done at the library. Aside from his steady job working for the railroad, he spent all of his spare time among his beloved books. At some point during this period, his interest turned to religious matters and the Unitarian faith. He then attended a Congregational preparatory school and became a Unitarian minister. After several postings in small towns in Minnesota and the Dakotas, he came to Alton in 1928. He always stated that his service in the Alton church was the happiest time that he had ever known. Then, in the early-morning hours of November 20, 1934, he committed suicide. The reason remains a mystery to this day.

Mercer's body was discovered by his friend James D. MaKinney, from whom the minister had rented a room in MaKinney's home at 319 East Fourth Street for nearly five years. MaKinney had been concerned when Mercer did not return home on Monday evening, but as the minister often attended concerts and musical events in St. Louis, he thought perhaps Mercer had spent the night in the city. By early afternoon, however, he began to get concerned.

As the day wore on, MaKinney grew worried. He began making telephone calls to the church, hoping to get in touch with Mercer, but there was no answer. Finally, just as it was getting dark, he decided to walk to the church and see if anyone was there. As he got close, he noticed that the lights were on in the rear rooms. He opened the west rear door and started inside, then saw Mercer hanging lifeless at the end of a rope. He ran across the street to the Alton Police Station and informed Desk Sergeant Scott of what he had seen. Patrolman Waller was assigned to accompany him back to the church. Once MaKinney confirmed that the body hanging from the transom was indeed his missing friend, Waller contacted the coroner and some of the church's trustees.

Mercer's body was taken down and removed to the Klunk Funeral Home, where visitations and a funeral service were held. His body was then placed in the Grandview Mausoleum to await instructions from his family in England. No instructions ever came though, and the body remains in the mausoleum to this day.

Why Phillip Mercer would have taken his own life remains as great a mystery as to where and how he spent the last hours of his life. No note or any other clue was found to explain why he would have taken his own life. The desk table in the minister's study was littered with papers, and it appeared as though someone had rummaged through them shortly before his death. Mercer had spoken little of personal or family matters, but he was an eager conversationalist and a seemingly happy and outgoing person who engaged his friends on current events, books, music, and entertainment. So what then would have caused his friends and congregation to believe that he had been the victim of a nervous breakdown?

According to James MaKinney, Mercer began to act rather strange a few months before. He became overly worried about his health and seemed to be obsessed with the idea that he was in bad physical condition. He started rapidly losing weight and complaining about feeling weak.

On the Sunday morning before his death, Mercer had conducted services at the church as usual. There was no indication that anything was troubling him, other than the fact that some members of the congregation reported that he read his sermon as if he were in a great hurry to get through it. They also said that he appeared to be sweating profusely, as if he were either sick or mentally agitated.

Two days later, he was discovered dead, but what could have driven him to take his own life? Was Phillip Mercer really ill, or was he mentally unbalanced? Another question that has been asked was whether Mercer may have led some sort of secret life. Could the stress of such a life have destroyed his health? Perhaps, for Mercer rarely discussed his personal life with anyone. In fact, after his death, a search through his personal papers revealed that Mercer was engaged to be married to a woman named Dorothy Cole of Minneapolis. In the six years that Mercer had been in Alton, he had never once mentioned her, nor did any of his friends or congregation members have any idea that she existed. When contacted by telegram, Miss Cole stated that Mercer had seemed depressed for some time and she had been trying to cheer him up with her letters, but her efforts had apparently failed.

What really happened to Phillip Mercer? There remain many more questions about his death, and his life, than there are answers, and these mysteries will likely never be solved. One of the most widely accepted theories of ghosts involves the personalities of those who once lived and have stayed behind in our world because of a murder, suicide, traumatic event, or some unfinished business in the person's life. If Phillip Mercer had some sort of unfinished business connecting him to the earth, whether it is a continuation of his good works or even the mysterious circumstances of his death, it is possible that his ghost has remained behind. And this might explain some of the strange things that have occurred at Alton's First Unitarian Church.

Over the years, there have been numerous reports of ghostly footsteps in the building, mysterious odors that come and go, doors that open and close, lights that turn on and off, strange sensations, and even the apparition of a man in the church sanctuary. Even church pastors often state that they feel they are not in the building alone.

The church can certainly be a place of peace, but for some of those who come here, it can be unnerving as well. It seems that someone lurks in this building, watching over the generations of parishioners who come here each week.

GHOSTS AND GOLD AT THE OLD STONE HOUSE

Along the Illinois River, and past the historic archaeological site near Kampsville, there are several small communities such as Eldred and Hillview. One of the most famous "lost" places in this region is the legendary Old Stone House. It is a place of murder, mystery, lost treasure—and perhaps even a ghost or two.

The Old Stone House was built in 1848 by Azariah Sweetin, a wealthy cattleman from Kentucky. Sweetin came to America from England, where he had been a stone mason. After moving to Illinois, he decided to build a magnificent mansion from the native stone on his new property. The lime was burned in kilns that were installed on the property, and limestone was then hewn into large blocks, creating three-foot-thick walls. The basement of the house was used for storage for grain and feed, and the living quarters were on the second floor. All of the woodwork was walnut, and a large tank that ran with natural spring water was used to cool the mansion, an early form of air-conditioning. The spring was piped into a large sink, and this was likely some of the first indoor plumbing in this area. The third floor was fashioned into a large ballroom, and special dances were held to celebrate the Fourth of July, Christmas, and New

Year's. Sweetin also installed two west windows in the third floor, which were kept lighted as a signal for steamboats, as there was a landing about 100 yards away from the house.

There are a number of legends about the house and the lost treasure that is still said to be hidden there today. The most famous story likely concerns the murder that occurred there around 1862. The tale has been altered and embellished over the years, but there is record that the homicide actually occurred— and that it left a "ghostly" impression behind.

Two men from the area came to the house in 1862 for a dance that was given for volunteers departing for the battlefields of the Civil War. A recruiting officer was in attendance in hopes that more of the local men would sign up. During the party, the sons of two local farmers began arguing, and the disagreement soon turned very heated. Finally, tired of bickering, one of the young men threw up his hands in disgust and walked away. When his back was turned, the other youth took a large knife from his belt and stabbed the departing young man in the back. He cried out in pain and then crumpled onto one of the mansion's fireplace hearths. He bled to death as he lay there on the rough stone.

According to legend, the impression of the young man's body appeared on the hearth a short time later. The blood that had been spilled there seeped into the stone in the perfect outline of the corpse and refused to be removed, no matter how much scrubbing was done. Writers mentioned seeing the bloodstains on the hearth in print as recently as 1936, and according to some, it remains there today—if you know where to look among the ruins of the house.

But this eerie impression is not the only strange tale of the Old Stone House. The greatest lingering mystery involves the lost treasure of Azariah Sweetin. Legend has it that the old man made a fortune trading cattle before the Civil War, but during the fighting, he lost faith in the banks and began hoarding all of his money around his property in gold coins. Some claimed that the coins were hidden in coffee cans, others in wooden chests. Or they may have been placed beneath the floorboards or secreted within the masonry of the fireplaces. No one knew for sure—including Azariah Sweetin himself. The story is that one day when Sweetin was out riding, he was thrown from his horse and hit his head. He was never the same again after that and could not remember where he had hidden his money. Although his family searched for it, they could not discover the hiding place.

A few years later, the Irving Wetzel family moved into the mansion, but when they left the property, the Old Stone House began to fall into ruin. Once the house was abandoned, local youths, treasure hunters, and curiosity seekers tore the place apart in a search for the lost gold. The mansion was nearly destroyed by the looting, but the gold was never found, leading many to believe that it was never hidden in the house at all, but rather in one of the caves in the bluff behind it. Searching for the treasure remains as hazardous today as it was at the turn of the last century, however, as rattlesnakes seek the shelter of the caves on hot afternoons. Many would-be gold seekers have retreated from the caves in fear after hearing the telltale sound of one of these deadly snakes.

And the rattlers are not, according to the legend, the only guardians of the gold. Some say the ghost of Azariah Sweetin lingers here too, watching over his treasure, having discovered in death what he lost in life.

SCHOOL SPIRIT AT LEWIS AND CLARK COLLEGE

Lewis and Clark College, or Monticello Seminary, as it was originally called, was founded in 1838 by Captain Benjamin Godfrey, a pioneer financier of the Alton area and a former sea captain. Captain Godfrey was a well-liked, adventurous man, and in light of his earlier career, it is somewhat surprising that he would found a college for females, especially at a time when it was almost unheard of for a woman to attend school at all. Godfrey was an uneducated Cape Cod shipmaster who had sailed the seven seas and had never seen the inside of a college building before coming to Alton. He did, however, have nine children, and one morning he overheard one of his daughters imitating her mother. As he then put it, "Educate a man and you educate an individual; educate a woman and you educate a family."

Godfrey had amassed a considerable fortune in real estate and railroad ownership when he decided to devote himself to the Monticello Female Seminary. He contributed more than $110,000 to the founding of the college and remained a trustee of the school until his death.

Godfrey chose the Reverend Theron Baldwin, a Yale-educated minister, to be the first principal of Monticello, which was now being called the "first female seminary in the west." Baldwin had also been instrumental in founding several other Midwestern colleges, including Illinois College at Jacksonville.

In 1838, most girls' schools were merely finishing schools that emphasized music, needlework, and other "womanly arts." The goal was a good marriage. At Monticello, however, the ladies were actually given a higher education, studying difficult courses in mathematics, English, history, religion, philosophy, foreign language, and music. The goal was still a good marriage, but the faculty at Monticello was determined the ladies would learn something as well.

For fifty years the plan flourished, right up until a terrible fire in 1888 that threatened to close the school for good. Two weeks later, though, rebuilding was already under way. The camaraderie between the students and the staff, created by the fire, intensified the school spirit and feeling of family at Monticello. This was a feeling that would last until the school closed down in 1971.

After Theron Baldwin retired, he was replaced by Miss Philomena Fobes, who continued the original plan for the school through the Civil War. As the college grew, it began to gain national notoriety and attracted students from all over the country. During the Civil War years, the campus became bitterly divided, as girls from both Union and Confederate families attended Monticello.

In 1867, however, Harriet Newell Haskell arrived as the new principal at Monticello and quickly mended the rift. She devoted the next forty years to making the school one of the most respected female institutions in the country, battling everything from a shortage of funds to the tragic fire of 1888.

Harriet Haskell was born in Waldoboro, Maine, in 1835. Always regarded as a tomboy, she was a favorite companion of both the boys and the girls of her neighborhood. She had a fertile imagination and was educated at Castleton Academy and Mount Holyoke, then went on to become the first female headmaster of the Franklin School in Boston. She was also named as president of Castleton, and when she was first asked to come to Monticello, she refused. Strangely, as the school later inspired so much devotion from her, she had visited the college and found that it wasn't to her liking. The Monticello board elected her to the job despite her refusal, and this time Miss Haskell accepted, perhaps seeing the school as a challenge that she could meet head-on.

The students at Monticello took to Miss Haskell right away, perhaps because of her wit and sharp sense of humor. She was also an early advocate of sports for women, believing that if they were well off physically, they would be fit emotionally and morally as well.

The great fire of 1888 became a history-making event for the school, and in lesser hands, the seminary would have closed down for good. For Harriet Haskell, though, it was merely a minor setback. When the fire was over, all that remained of the "first female seminary in the west" was a pile of smoldering embers and a hollowed-out and blackened shell that was once the tower. Later that morning, a large wagon loaded with empty trunks arrived, and the ladies were instructed to choose one and place their salvaged possessions inside. The trunks were then shipped home. One of the trunks, belonging to a young lady who followed Miss Haskell's instructions to the letter, had only a single rubber boot inside. The ladies were all sent home, and as they departed, they looked back to see Miss Haskell standing on the college lawn, staring at what remained of the beloved school. Few of them honestly believed that they would ever see the seminary, or Harriet Haskell, again.

But anyone who thought the school would close down had sorely underestimated the iron will of Miss Haskell. She immediately began a spectacular fundraising campaign for the school, collecting thousands of dollars and launching a new building called Caldwell Hall, which was designed by the architect of Union Station in St. Louis, Theodore Link. In a short time, the college was up and running again, and by 1902, Miss Haskell announced that the college was officially out of debt.

Although she never married, Miss Haskell raised two nieces and purchased a Federal-style home on campus, called the Evergreens, in the 1890s. Many students at Monticello left with the feeling that Miss Haskell had loved them as much as she would have her own children.

Miss Haskell's reign at Monticello Seminary endured for forty years, and her tenure as the head of the college was the school's highest point, by both educational and financial standards. She had a real knack for securing donations for the school and was respected by parents and board members alike. She was also adored by the students, and when she died, the Haskell Girls, as they called themselves, were deeply grieved. Former students from across the country sent flowers and cards and came from great distances to attend her funeral.

The tenure of Miss Catherine Burrowes followed, but things were never the same for many of the girls. The school did not again achieve the fame that it had when Harriet Haskell was alive. It did continue to grow and prosper for some time, although eventually time and coeducational colleges caught up with the school. The last class graduated from Monticello in 1971, and the campus became the home of Lewis and Clark Community College. Much of the campus has since been renovated. What used to be dorm rooms are now offices, and the old school chapel is now a library.

Though things have changed at the college, others have remained the same. One of those things is the presence of Harriet Haskell. Her days at Monticello may have ended in 1907—but some people insist that she is still present, at least in spirit.

The stories about Harriet Haskell's ghost began long ago, shortly after her death in 1907. At the time, Monticello girls were scaring the new students with tales of Miss Haskell's ghost, wandering up and down the hallways at night. Others told of seeing her face reflected in mirrors and apparitions in darkened corridors. Were the ghostly tales of Harriet Haskell merely legends to frighten new arrivals at the school? Perhaps—or perhaps not. Along with these chilling stories were events not so easy to explain away. The oldest house on campus had lights and fountains that periodically turned on and off by themselves. The steam-operated elevator in the old administration building would suddenly start up and run by itself. The security guards would discover that no one was in it, but it would mysteriously travel between floors at night. As time passed, more and more people were experiencing odd occurrences and even seeing apparitions of Miss Haskell. Others were reporting that lights were turning on in empty rooms at night and that water would sometimes run in the bathrooms for no reason.

It seems that one of the most haunted places on campus is the library, which was once the Monticello chapel, said to be Miss Haskell's favorite room. Compulsory chapel was held each day in this incredibly beautiful place. It is in this room where the spirit of Harriet Haskell is encountered the most. Many report having smelled the overwhelming fragrance of lilac perfume—Miss Haskell's trademark scent, which appears to signal that her presence is near.

But does it really? Several generations of students believe that it does, and they will tell you that Harriet Haskell is never far away from the school that she loved so much.

THE HAUNTED RUEBEL HOTEL

The steamboat era was ushered into the small town of Grafton in 1844 and became the most exciting time in the city's history. The railroad joined the riverboats in the 1880s, and during its peak, three separate lines came into town, making it a rough and often rollicking place. In addition to the railroad and the river men who came to town, many respectable travelers passed through Grafton as well and were in need of a decent place to spend the night. Talk began to spread about the possibility of a grand hotel.

Michael Ruebel built the Ruebel Hotel in 1884, and it has become known as the most haunted location in Grafton. When it opened, it was the largest commercial hotel in Jersey County. It had thirty-two rooms, with a bathhouse in the back, and mainly played host to river travelers. Room rates at the time were $1 per day. Weekly rooms could be had for a rate of $8 and included three meals a day.

The hotel also boasted the finest saloon in town, at a time when twenty-six saloons operated in Grafton. Needless to say, this was a rowdy place to be, but with a population made up of mainly Irish and German quarry workers, who were used to brawling and drinking contests, the large number of saloons became a necessity. Because of its reputation on the river, the Ruebel Hotel was also frequently visited by river travelers and steamboat operators, further adding to the colorful atmosphere. The hotel thrived until 1912, when it was damaged by fire. It was quickly rebuilt, however, this time with a restaurant on the first floor and a dance hall on the second. During World War II, the dance hall was turned into quarters for thirty Coast Guard men, who were stationed in Grafton to provide protection for the river traffic.

As time went on, the rest of the world passed Grafton by. After two world wars, the Great Depression, floods, the end of the steamboat era, and the closing of the local rail lines, the town slowly withered. And the Ruebel Hotel died along with it. By the 1980s, the building had become an abandoned derelict, its heyday long forgotten. Then in 1996, the hotel was purchased by the Jeff Lorton family, who completely restored the place and opened it for business in the spring of 1997.

Shortly after the Ruebel reopened, at least three guests and a hotel housekeeper reported encountering a ghost in the building. In April 1997, these overnight guests told the owners the next morning that they had spoken to the ghost of a little girl named Abigail. Since then, a number of other folks who have spent the night in the hotel say they too have seen a young girl in the upstairs hallway and at the top of the stairway to the second floor.

THE LEGEND OF THE HARTFORD CASTLE

Once located near the small town of Hartford, where the Mississippi and Missouri Rivers merge, was a magnificent mansion that the locals called Hartford Castle. It is a house that has been plagued with rumors of murder, of bootleg liquor, and especially, of ghosts. Much of the history of the castle—which was officially known as Lake View—has been lost, or in many cases, never existed at all. It was a house built for love, that became overshadowed by grief, despair, and the bizarre—and it became a place of mystery. It seems that what the locals didn't know about the castle and its eccentric owner, they simply made up. But, as we will soon see, truth is often stranger than fiction.

Lakeview was built by J. J. Bizsant, a real estate investor and contractor from Los Angeles. No one seems to know why he chose to build his lavish estate near Hartford, but he originally intended it to be a summer home for himself and his English wife. Possessing perhaps more money than good sense, he designed Lake View as homage to his wife's home country with towers, turrets, and even a castle moat that was dug by workers with teams of horses. The excavated earth was used to create the knoll on which the house was built, looming high enough that Bizsant and his bride could look out over the countryside from their third-floor windows.

When the castle was completed, it could be seen from the distant road. It had fourteen rooms, numerous fireplaces, and even its own water and electrical plant on the grounds. The floors were made of imported cypress wood and the ceilings supported by hand-carved columns. Crystal chandeliers were used in mirror-lined main hall and music could often be heard drifting out over the fields in the evening.

But it was the grounds of the estate that really got the locals talking. Bizsant dug a fifty-foot moat that surrounded the estate. The only access to the grounds was by means of a drawbridge over the moat. The drawbridge wasn't difficult to cross, but once on the other side of it, a visitor would be confronted by a labyrinth of walks and gravel paths that weaved throughout the grounds. The gardens were decorated with gazeboes and statues of all types, including those of fierce-looking dogs, which lined the moats and menaced from the bushes. A stone bridge was built to reach an island in the middle of the small lakes that adjoined the moat and the lakes were used for swimming. Bizsant kept them all stocked with goldfish.

Lake View became the scene of exclusive parties that lasted long into the night and sometimes until dawn. Stories circulated about Bizsant's spectacular billiards room and about the high-stakes card games that often took place. Music, voices, and laughter echoed out across the surrounding fields and lights could be seen blazing in the house from miles away.

Locals were scandalized by the wild parties that allegedly took place at the castle. Stories spread of strange things that occurred during those illicit nights—drinking, gambling, dancing, and crazed orgies. The *St. Louis Star* newspaper hinted that there might be a social upheaval in St. Louis if the identity of some of those who visited Lake View became public knowledge. The paper also went on to say that the honest and plain-spoken farm families of the area were so shocked that they threatened to burn the house to the ground.

But the threats became unnecessary because one day, the parties simply stopped.

The castle that had once been filled with music and lights became silent and dark. The gates were locked, the curtains were closed, and soon, it appeared that Lake View had been abandoned. A pall fell over the castle with the death of Bizsant's beloved wife. Unable to cope with the loss, he closed the house and returned to California. Over the next few years, he returned infrequently, too grief-stricken to spend much time at the castle that he had built for the woman he loved and lost. The newspapers claimed that Bizsant became involved with a group of Spiritualist mediums in Los Angeles, all who promised the wealthy man that they could contact his wife. Bizsant continued his search for proof of life after death for the rest of his life and he died in California in the 1920s.

Did he ever contact his late wife? We'll never know, but if he didn't, it's perhaps because he was looking in the wrong place. It seems that Mrs. Bizsant may have never left Lake View.

In the years that followed the abandonment of the castle, more strange stories began to be told about the place. Locals refused to set foot on the grounds because they were sure the place was haunted. Lights were often reported flicking behind the windows, even though no one lived in the castle now. Bizsant had locked the place up tight before departing and had left the estate in the care of an old German named Henry Meyer, who never went inside unless he had to.

The strange happenings were the work of the ghost of Mrs. Bizsant, locals said, refusing to leave the elaborate castle that her husband had built for her.

In 1913, the stories of Lake View's hauntings spread throughout the region when newspapers reported an attempted burglary that occurred at the house in March of that year. The house wasn't actually robbed. The thief never had the chance to steal anything, he claimed, because he was terrified by the ghost.

In time, the house was sold, but the ghost stories never really stopped. They continued to be told through various owners, even until the very end of the castle's existence. Over the years, they became jumbled and half-remembered, as did the origins of the magnificent—and mysterious—house.

Sadly, much of the specific history of the castle has been lost. We are left with only vague records and recollections of its many owners and the many things it was used for. Fact seems to blend with fiction, and we can never be sure just how accurate many of the stories are.

In the twentieth century, there were stories that Lakeview was a boy's military school and a home for unwed mothers. In the 1920s, it became an inn that also operated as a speakeasy during the Prohibition era. While a rumor, it is a plausible one. The house was isolated enough that it would've kept party-goers and gangsters from being bothered by the law. Rumor has it that the booze at Lake View was provided by local gangsters but, of course, no one can say for sure.

What we do know is that Lake View was purchased by a couple from nearby Wood River, Illinois, in the early 1930s. They lived in the house until 1964. Soon after moving in, they began to be bothered by intruders and trespassers. The castle had been around so long that many in the area treated the grounds like a public park. People roamed the estate at all hours of the day and night. Some even broke into the house and wandered from room to room, as if they were on a tour. After finding strangers camped out in their front yard too many times to count, the couple finally decided to open the grounds for picnics on weekends, hoping this would curb the break-ins and vandalism. It didn't help. They posted "no trespassing" signs but they didn't do much good either.

In 1964, the owner died, and his widow moved back to Wood River. There were attempts to rent the house after that, hoping that someone would just remain on the grounds to protect it from vandalism, but it never worked out. After 1964, upkeep on the house and property came to an end and the estate crumbled into ruin. By 1972, the castle—after years of damage from thieves and vandals—was beyond saving, especially after intruders gutted the place, ripped mantels from the fireplaces, broke the remaining windows, and smashed huge holes in the interior walls. Lake View was officially condemned by county inspectors.

The end came for the Hartford Castle on March 21, 1973, when it burned to the ground. An alarm was raised by a motorist driving past, but by the time that firefighter arrived on the scene, only a tall chimney and burning embers remained of the castle.

Lake View was destroyed, but believe it or not, parts of it still remain. The once grand estate has been swallowed by a cluster of thick woods and brambles, not far from Hartford. Remnants of the castle exist as broken stone columns, shattered statues, a concrete gazebo, and the dim impression of the estate's once infamous moat.

But that's not all, there are also the legends—and there is also the ghost.

The site of the Hartford Castle may be haunted by history, but it is haunted by the ghost of Bizsant's wife, as well. There are those who say that her spectral form can still sometimes be spotted wandering the estate and that her voice can still be heard as she weeps for the life and the wonderful home that she lost.

And then there is the music. They say that on certain nights, it can still be heard. It floats through the trees and above the fields on summer nights when the corn grows tall and when sounds seem to carry for miles. Perhaps, in another time and place, Lake View still stands. And the party still goes on.

THE PHANTOM FUNERAL OF FORT DE CHARTRES

Along an old road near the sleepy Southwestern Illinois town of Prairie du Rocher, the heartland's most famous phantom funeral procession is said to walk each year that Independence Day falls on a Friday. The legend of the phantom funeral began in July 1889, when two women reported witnessing a mourning entourage of more than forty wagons, thirteen groups of soldiers, and a casket rolling along the road outside of the village. Despite the size of the group, the procession made no sound. It left the ruins of old Fort de Chartres and disappeared in the direction of the small cemetery located outside town. Although they did not yet realize it, the women, as well as one other witness, had glimpsed what has become known as one of the most famous enduring mysteries of the Mississippi River region.

The first settlers in the southern portion of Illinois were the French, who established trading posts and settlements in places such as Kaskaskia and Cahokia, near the Mississippi River. Not far from the present-day town of Prairie du Rocher is the site of the state's earliest military post, Fort de Chartres, which has a rich, violent, and bloody history.

Several different forts stood at the site, the first built around 1720. The area was beginning to be settled by this time, and the French were laying claim to as much land as possible. The fort became an outfitting location for further colonization. In 1751, an Irish soldier of fortune named Richard MacCarty became commander of the French fort. The original fort had fallen into ruin, and it was his responsibility to construct a new one using slave labor and local limestone. The new fort took three years to build and cost over $1 million, an enormous expense at that time. When completed, it could house 400 soldiers and enclosed an area of more than 4 acres. It also boasted a powder magazine, storehouse, prison with four dungeons, barracks, and officers' quarters.

After France's defeat in the French and Indian War, the Illinois Territory was ceded to Britain in 1763. The Indians, led by Chief Pontiac, were hostile to the new British rulers, however, and two years passed before the English could take possession of Fort de Chartres. Under British command, the fort declined and fell into ruin. Many of the French farmers and merchants migrated west across the Mississippi during the British years, abandoning the area. To make matters worse, a river flood in 1772 damaged the fort and left seven feet of water standing inside the walls. Finally, the river channel shifted, and the west wall of the structure collapsed. After this, the military garrison was transferred to Kaskaskia, and Fort de Chartres was never occupied again.

As time wore on, the ruins fell apart, and birds began nesting in the crumbling stone. The site was largely forgotten until the middle 1900s, when historic restoration efforts began. Today the original foundations have been exposed, and a few of the old buildings have been restored. Living-history groups frequent the place, and visitors are invited to this isolated place to learn about the earliest settlements in Illinois.

But it seems that the events of the past never died completely at Fort de Chartres, and it is said that at least one of them replays over and over again in the form of a phantom funeral procession that has become one of the most famous haunts in Southern Illinois. According to the legend, whenever the Fourth of July falls on a Friday, three people along the road from Fort de Chartres to a small cemetery in Prairie du Rocher will be able to witness the funeral procession between the hours of eleven and midnight.

The modern version of this intriguing story begins in July 1889. A woman named Mrs. Chris was sitting on the front porch of her house near Prairie du Rocher with her neighbor one night. It was near midnight, and the two women had escaped the heat of the house by going out into the cooler air on the porch. They talked quietly for a short time, and then one of the women noticed a large group of people coming toward them on the road. She caught the attention of her friend, and they puzzled over why such a procession of people and wagons would be on the road from the old fort at such an hour. As they spoke, the wagons rolled into view, looking strange and eerie in the pale light of the moon. Behind the wagons came carriages and men and women walking along the dusty road. There was no clue as to their purpose on this night, until a low wagon holding a casket came into view. It was apparently a funeral procession, Mrs. Chris thought, but why so late at night?

As the two women continued to watch, they counted nearly forty wagons, followed by horsemen and mourners on foot. Then they noticed something very peculiar about the grim parade. Even though the wagon wheels seemed to pound the earth and the feet of the men and women stirred up clouds of dust, none of them made any sound at all. The entire procession was impossibly silent. The only sounds came from the rustling of the trees in the breeze and the incessant barking of the Chris family dog, which also sensed that something was not quite right with the spectral and silent procession. The barking of the dog awakened the neighbor woman's husband, who looked out and also witnessed the strange entourage on the road. He verified the women's account early the next morning, but other than these three people, no one else saw the phantom funeral march.

Eventually the procession passed by and faded away into the darkness. The two women waited the entire night for the funeral to return, but they saw nothing more. What was it that they had seen, and whose funeral was being conducted? The answers came some years later, and they learned that the procession apparently had also been seen in the past.

During the French occupation of Fort de Chartres, the story goes, a prominent local man had gotten into a violent disagreement with one of the officers of the garrison. The two men exchanged heated words, and the local merchant was accidentally killed. Unsure of how to handle the affair, the fort's commander sent a delegation to the government offices in Kaskaskia. They advised keeping the incident very quiet and ordered that the local man be buried at midnight in the small cemetery now outside Prairie du Rocher. Whether this event really occurred or not, the truth behind the story has been obscured by legend. It seems, however, that Mrs. Chris and her neighbors were witnesses to an inexplicable event that was replayed more than a century after it first occurred. Since 1889, accounts have been sketchy, but some have claimed that the phantom funeral continues to be seen.

Intrigued by the tale? You will have the chance to search for the phantom funeral on your own in the future. July 4 will again fall on a Friday in the years 2008, 2014, and 2025. If you are feeling brave, take along two friends and stake out the old road that leads to Fort de Chartres. You might just be in the right place at the right time when the dead decide to walk once more.

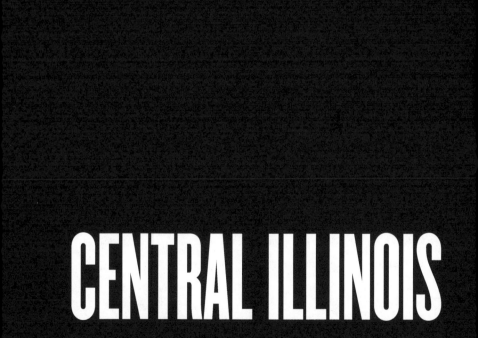

CENTRAL ILLINOIS

For the last several decades or so, the main way of life in Central Illinois has been built around farming, but it was not always this way. In fact, when the early settlers came here, they chose to live in the shelter of the forests that grew along the nearby sources of water. The vast prairie land that stretched before them was both inviting and frightening, and it was some years to come before the waves of grass and rich ground were broken to eke out an existence from the soil. These first settlers were mostly hunters, with a few farmers mixed in, and all of them made their homes on the edge of the timber. They did not realize for some time that there was nothing wrong with the Central Illinois soil. They didn't understand how soil that grew prairie grass, yet no trees, could possibly be fertile. In addition, the trees were essential for survival, providing wood for fires, tools, and, especially, homes in which to live. When most of the populace turned to farming, they found that wooden split-rail fences protected the fields and kept the livestock from roaming into the forest and being killed by wolves.

The farmers soon found that corn was an ideal crop for the prairie. It was easy to sow, cultivate, and turn into many food products and a marketable whiskey. Many farmers owned stills that converted corn mash into a clear but potent whiskey that could then be transported to market via packhorse or river barge. This corn alcohol became a popular western drink, and jugs circulated freely at social events like dances, barn raisings, and especially at election time.

The secondary crop became wheat, which could be converted to flour, but only at a mill. The mills came a little later, following the small settlements, and brought rudimentary mechanics to the frontier. The mills were built along rivers for power, but where dams could not be constructed, horses and oxen turned the grinding stones. Soon the mill became the leading establishment in many of the settlements, and other businesses, such as blacksmith shops and general stores, followed closely behind.

In those days, almost no one on the prairie had money. The settlers made their own clothing. The men tanned the hides of deer and cattle for shoes, and the women made trousers, shirts, and dresses with spinning wheels and looms. They grew their own food or hunted it in the forests, and the small farms provided eggs, milk, and butter. In the general stores, the settlers could trade any surplus goods for whiskey, sugar, salt, tools, crockery, or coffee.

But as idyllic as this all sounds, the frontier was not without its dangers—often, in the early years, from the Native American populace. The Kickapoo and other tribes kept the settlers in a constant state of alarm for many years. Pioneers also died from the many diseases that plagued the region, as well as from the often extreme weather conditions. Terrible thunderstorms on the open plains were not uncommon, and fires were frequently started by lightning strikes, which could burn whole fields, stands of woods, or even entire towns. Life on the prairie was not easy, and the strange tales of days gone by apparently have given birth to many hauntings.

THE HAUNTING OF THE COLISEUM BALLROOM

Located along the original alignment of Route 66 through Central Illinois was the legendary Coliseum Ballroom. The ballroom's long and often mysterious past has been linked to big band history, bootlegging, gangsters, murder, and more, and it was one of the great old landmarks of the region for many years. The ballroom stopped being a dancehall a few decades before the fatal fire that destroyed it in 2011, but it still managed to attract people from all over the region who came looking for a little history—and for its resident ghosts.

The Coliseum Ballroom was opened on December 24, 1924, for the grand sum of more than $50,000. This was not only an astronomical amount for the time period, but it was also an exorbitant expense for the little village of Benld, a rough mining community that was better known for its bars and brothels than for its musical entertainment. The ballroom was built and operated by Dominick Tarro, a local businessman, but rumors spread that the funding for the project had come from unsavory pockets, namely those of gangsters who planned to use the ballroom as a warehouse for illegal liquor between Chicago and St. Louis.

And as it turned out, the rumors apparently had some basis in truth. In January 1930, Tarro was arrested as the leader of the bootlegging operation in Benld. Many believed that he planned to cooperate with the authorities in exchange for leniency, and it was no surprise when he disappeared shortly after posting bond for his release. His body turned up on May 5 of that year in the Sangamon River. Heavy wire had been bound around his neck and hands, and he had been shot in the back of the head.

Following his death, Tarro's wife, Marie, took over management of the ballroom. In the years that followed, the Coliseum gained legendary status for the big-name groups that were booked here. The ballroom drew top talent of all types, dating from the 1930s all the way into the 1970s. Some of the bands and acts that played here included Guy Lombardo, Sammy Kaye, Tommy Dorsey, Count Basie, Lawrence Welk, Duke Ellington, Lionel Hampton, Ray Charles, Ike and Tina Turner, Fats Domino, Chuck Berry, Chubby Checker, the Everly Brothers, Jerry Lee Lewis, Bill Haley and the Comets, Fleetwood Mac, Ted Nugent, and Bob Seger. People came from all over the region, even the state, to see the acts Marie and later her daughter Joyce booked into the Coliseum. The ballroom had the largest dance floor in the state of Illinois, outside of Chicago, and could seat as many as 800 people on the main floor and in the balcony.

The place enjoyed great success for many years, especially after Joyce Tarro took over operations. She was a tough, hardheaded businesswoman who had a habit of carrying the weekend receipts around with her all the time. She was known to pack a revolver in the waistband of her slacks, but this didn't deter two people from breaking into her home in February 1976 and waiting for her to return. When Joyce came in and discovered the intruders, she managed to fire a few shots at them, but she tragically was shot and died. This second violent death brought down the curtain on the Tarro era at the Coliseum.

The ballroom struggled for a few years but was never the same after Joyce's death. Times turned tough. New owners attempted to revitalize the place a time or two with music acts and even as a roller rink, but it never again enjoyed the success of its earlier days. However, it was during these days of decline that employees began to report strange incidents in the building. Eerie footsteps were often heard, and shadowy figures were sometimes reported in dark corners. One former employee, George Luttman, who worked there from 1977 to 1981, told me that he often came in to clean in the mornings and on several occasions he saw people in formal clothes who looked as if they were ready to swing to the sounds of Tommy Dorsey or one of the other big bands of the era. When approached, the figures always vanished.

The Coliseum fell into years of abandonment and further decline, but then, in the late 1990s, it was reopened as an antique mall and a roadside attraction on Route 66. The new owners bought the building in October and had a lot of work to do before they could make their planned opening in February. Almost immediately, they later reported, a woman was spotted upstairs who should not have been there. The figure had short dark hair and was there one moment and then gone the next. No one had any idea who she might be, but she was seen in the building many times after that.

Customers, visitors, and even antique dealers who came in to stock their booths reported a litany of odd happenings. A local carpenter, who helped renovate the building, saw a man ascend a back stairway that the owners had blocked for safety reasons. When the carpenter went up the rickety stairs to investigate, he found that the opening of the stairs was inaccessible. There was no way that anyone could have climbed up the staircase.

Dealers and customers experienced cold spots among the booths and in hallways and told of a misty woman who was often seen near a former bar area. In spite of the fact that the owners paid to have the place re-wired, lights frequently turned on and off without explanation. Others told of feeling a presence as the hair on the backs of their necks stood on end. They also talked of a breeze that moved past them as if someone had just walked by. In every case, no one visible was near.

Eventually, the owners closed the Coliseum. Likely discouraged by the lack of traffic that ventured off the interstate, they moved their operations a few miles south to a former school building in Livingston. The Coliseum was closed, dark, and empty for several years, but then reopened again, first as an antique mall and then as a venue for live music once again. It seemed that things were finally starting to happen again at the legendary ballroom, but then disaster struck. On July 31, 2011, a fire broke out during a music show and the Coliseum was gutted by flames. The building was beyond repair, marking the end of a small piece of Central Illinois' haunted history.

THE GHOST OF MARY HAWKINS

Pemberton Hall at Eastern Illinois University was the first college building in Illinois to provide housing for young women on campus. This radical new idea was first proposed in 1901 but was quickly denied. It took six more years and the backing of Senator Stanton C. Pemberton before the new hall could be built and named in the senator's honor. It housed up to 100 women and Miss Estelle Gross became the first headmistress. She only served in that position for one year before being succeeded by the most infamous name in the building's history, Mary Elizabeth Hawkins.

Mary Hawkins was born in Moat, a small town in Northern England, almost on the border with Scotland. She came to America in 1901 at the age of twenty-four. Not much is known about her life in the United States, until 1910, when she assumed the position of dorm director at Pemberton Hall. She was not a beloved figure by the young women under her charge. She imposed strict rules and curfews on the residents. Class and church services were the only places that the women were allowed to go unchaperoned. However, they were free to go home on weekends and allowed to entertain guests on Saturday and Sunday evenings until 10:00 p.m.

Mary continued to serve the school for the next several years, but in early 1917, her mental health began to deteriorate. She left her position at Pemberton Hall in March of that year and as her condition worsened, she spent two weeks at the M. A. Montgomery Memorial Sanitarium in Charleston in September 1918. According to doctors, she was "depressed and irrational," accompanied by hallucinations, insomnia, and memory loss. They believed that she was suffering from "overwork and over worry." She died on the night of October 29, 1918, at the Kankakee State Mental Hospital. Hospital orderlies discovered her body the next morning. Mary's death certificate listed the cause of death as "general paralysis of the insane." She was buried in Charleston's Mound Cemetery and two years after her death, the university hung a bronze tablet that commemorated her service to the school.

Life at Pemberton Hall continued without Mary Hawkins. As time passed, it's likely that she would have largely been forgotten, barely remembered as a name on a memorial plaque that still hangs near the entrance. But, at some point, the story of Mary Hawkins became part of the legend of Pemberton Hall. It's unknown today how folklore and history merged to create the tale of the residence hall's ghost, but she has been a very real part of the fabric of the place.

For nearly a century, the ghost of Mary Hawkins has haunted Pemberton Hall. Or has she? The truth of the story is a bit of a mystery. There are dozens of variations of the story of how Mary Hawkins's ghost ended up haunting Pemberton Hall, including a "murdered coed" story that claimed a girl was killed in the attic music room. Her body was discovered by Mary Hawkins, the legend said, who, after being driven insane, committed suicide.

Soon after the murder and suicide, the residents of Pemberton Hall started to report strange occurrences in the building—spooky events that continue to this day. They believed the incidents could be explained as the ghost of Mary Hawkins, still making her rounds, and checking in on the young women who lived in the building. Perhaps her spirit was unable to rest after losing one of the women in her care and she roamed the hall after death, watching out for them, and protecting them from harm. The spirit would glide through the rooms, lock and unlock doors, turn off radios and lights, and generally keep track of the things that went on in the hall.

The ghost stories first appeared in print in 1976 but had been around for years. Young women were awakened at all hours of the night by banging on the doors and knocks that seemed to be coming from inside of the walls. No cause was ever determined for the string of bizarre incidents. Most assumed that it was the resident ghost, trying to make her presence known.

In the 1960s and early 1970s, residents reported hearing whispers in the building, especially on the fourth floor, and there were a number of reports of an apparition on the stairway. The figure appeared very briefly and then vanished. In the 1976 account by Karen Knupp, she recalled the problems that the resident advisors had with the furniture in one of the lounges. It seemed that all the furniture in this room was often found to be overturned or, at the very least, rearranged. It often happened during the overnight hours, but not always. One morning, an Resident Advisor walked into the room and discovered that all of the furniture had been moved around—chairs were turned backward, the couch moved out of the corner, a table was blocking the door—and she assumed that someone had been playing a prank on her. She went to get some help to straighten up the room and when she and another resident came back, they found that everything had been restored to order. After that, the RA just always left the room in whatever state she found it and, somehow, it would always be cleaned up again. The students on the floor all denied knowing how this continued to take place.

In 1984, the *Decatur Herald & Review* published an account by Patty O'Neill, who had lived in Pemberton Hall for three years. She had been up late studying one night in the spring of 1981. She was in one of the lounges and eventually returned to her room to go to bed. Her roommate was already asleep when she came in and rather than slam the door closed to lock it, she decided to just pull it closed and leave it unlocked for the night. This was a common occurrence because the old door was slightly wider than the frame and had to be pulled hard to close it.

Patty climbed into bed and drifted off to sleep. She had not been sleeping long before she was startled awake. She wasn't sure what had awakened her at first, but then she realized that the room was freezing. She reached out for a blanket, but then stopped suddenly. She saw a woman in a long white nightgown standing at the end of her bed. The woman stood there for a few seconds, and then she turned and walked toward the door. Patty noted in her story, "She opened the door and started to leave and then she turned, with one hand on the door, and looked back at me for several seconds. She then left, closing the door behind her."

And Patty's room was not the only one visited by this nocturnal specter. As the apparition had left the room, she had locked the door behind her. Strangely, several other residents, who distinctly remembered leaving their doors open, also found them to be mysteriously locked the next morning. Patty surmised that the spirit had been checking on them and had been worried about their safety. The implication was that it was the ghost of Mary Hawkins.

According to Michelle Mueller in the *Daily Eastern News*, another chilling event occurred in 1984. A resident at Pemberton Hall discovered small, black footprints on the floor of her room. The prints appeared to be from someone who had tip-toed across the room. They led from the door to the closet, and then back out of the room again. Was it a prank? No one knows, but the prints proved to be impossible to remove.

By the 1990s, events were taking place at Pemberton Hall that convinced even the most skeptical of residents that the place was truly haunted. On many occasions, there were firsthand reports of late-night door knocking and inexplicable sounds in the halls. When doors were opened to see who might be there, the corridor was always found to be empty. On other occasions, residents claimed to find clothing had been removed from their locked rooms at night and then had been thrown haphazardly up and down the halls.

As the years have passed, the story of Pemberton Hall and its resident ghost lives on at Eastern Illinois University. The jumbled legends of Mary Hawkins and the murdered young student are still told, and tales still circulate about the sounds of a piano playing in the fourth-floor music room. The question remains as to the identity of the ghost who haunts this building—but there is no question to most students that someone does. The spirit has been here for a very long time and seems to be content to linger for a few decades more.

THE CHESTERVILLE WITCH'S GRAVE

Chesterville is a small town that no longer appears on most maps of the state. The village still exists, though, and is located just west of Arcola, which is in the heart of Illinois Amish country. Most of the remaining residents of the town are of Amish and Mennonite religious orders that shun the use of electricity and modern conveniences.

Located just outside the village, and across an ancient one-lane bridge, is the small Chesterville Cemetery. It is in this secluded graveyard that a traveler can find what is said to be a witch's grave. According to the legend, the grave belongs to a young woman who once lived in Chesterville and was regarded as a witch in the community, although her name is no longer recalled. Her ghost is rumored to still appear nearby. The woman was very liberal-minded and liked to challenge the Amish faith, speaking out against the treatment of women in the area. Thanks to this, she was branded a witch. She continued to disobey the elders of the church and was banished. As few ever questioned the decisions made by the church elders, rumors quickly spread through the community that she practiced witchcraft, was a servant of the devil, and worse. Soon after, she disappeared.

A short time later, the woman was discovered dead in a farmer's field. Although no one really knew what had happened, the authorities ruled that her death was from natural causes. Her remains were placed in the local funeral home, and people from all over the countryside came to view the "witch's body." They were terrified that she would come back to life.

Eventually she was buried in the Chesterville Cemetery, and a tree was planted on her grave so that her spirit would be trapped in the tree. Today that tree remains standing, and many still believe that if the tree ever dies or is cut down, the witch's spirit will escape and take her revenge on the town. A fence was later placed around the grave site to make sure that people stayed away from it.

Since that time, the witch has allegedly appeared to passersby and visitors to the cemetery, although thanks to the tree, she is confined to the area around her grave. A number of stories have been told about this cemetery involving sightings and reports that have led some to believe the legend of the Chesterville witch may not be just a folk tale after all.

PHANTOMS OF THE LINCOLN THEATER

The Lincoln Theater opened with great fanfare in downtown Decatur in October 1916, to standing-room-only crowds of the city's finest citizens, dressed in black tie and formal wear and eager to see the new, glorious theater they had heard so much about. The first program to be presented was George M. Cohan's stage comedy Hit-the-Trail Holliday, starring Frank Otto. The audience loved the show and raved about the spectacular design of the theater, with its private seating boxes, massive ivory-colored columns, and 1,346 seats, all of which offered a splendid view and wonderful acoustics. Also new to Decatur was the mezzanine seating, which ran just below the balcony and provided seats that were only slightly above the level of the stage.

In those early years, the main emphasis at the Lincoln was on stage shows and vaudeville acts. Many famous stars appeared here, including Ethel Barrymore, Al Jolson, Ed Wynn, and Jeanette MacDonald. Audiences also thrilled to such attractions as a sparring exhibition by Jack Dempsey after his famous fight with Georges Carpentier.

In February 1926, the theater hired a twelve-member orchestra to provide music for all stage productions and the silent films that were starting to gain popularity. Vaudeville remained the most popular attraction the theater had to offer, however, and the orchestra's leader brought a young, unknown comedian named Bob Hope to the Lincoln in 1926 to show Decatur how to dance the Charleston. Hope was just starting his career in those days, and he returned often during the 1920s to appear in vaudeville shows and comedy productions.

Moving pictures continued to increase in popularity in the city, and Decatur's residents were demanding more and more films to take the place of stage shows. In April 1928, the first "talkies" came to Decatur and played at the Empress Theater. The Lincoln began showing them fourteen months later, at the close of the vaudeville season. This heralded the end of the vaudeville days at the Lincoln, and perhaps in the entire city. Sound equipment was installed in the theater for films, making silent movies obsolete, and bandleader Billy Gail and his orchestra were promptly dismissed.

The theater operated steadily for many years, but by the late 1970s, it had fallen on hard times. By 1980, it was closed down, sadly destined to become an aging relic in Decatur's fading downtown business district. The Lincoln remained dark for many years, opening only occasionally for live music and barely attended events. By 1990, the building had deteriorated badly and was suffering from neglect.

Thankfully, the Lincoln came to the attention of a restoration group, and some life has been brought back to the old place. Thousands of dollars and countless hours of work have been put into the theater, but it still has a long way to go. The restoration effort has been a lengthy and painfully slow project, with possibly many years remaining before it will be completed. This has not stopped many local and national groups from performing here, however, and many times during these performances, regular people have encountered things in the theater than can only be described as something well beyond the ordinary.

Stories have circulated about a haunting at the Lincoln Theater since at least the 1930s. Reports by witnesses from those early days of film in the theater suggested that at least one ghost haunts the building. In more recent times, the numerous encounters there have led many to believe that a multitude of spirits may linger in the Lincoln. One of the ghosts appears to be that of a stagehand who died in the building during the vaudeville days, but there may be many others.

Over the years, dozens of witnesses have said they heard strange sounds and footsteps in the otherwise empty theater—and these sounds could not be explained away as simply caused by the theater's acoustics. People have also reported whispers, strange voices, and even a shadowy apparition in the theater's balcony. In addition to the visual sightings and sounds, there have been a number of other encounters as well. Many have experienced inexplicable cold chills in certain spots in the building, and others claim to have been touched by unseen hands. Several others have mentioned seeing theater seats in the auditorium raise and lower by themselves, as if an unseen audience were watching the show.

Other supernatural incidents have occurred around what may be the most haunted spot in the theater—a metal spiral staircase at the back corner of the stage. Many witnesses claim to have had unearthly encounters on and around the staircase. For example, in 1994, an entertainer who was performing in a traveling production reported that he saw a man lurking on this staircase. He was in the back corner changing his costume when he heard a voice whispering to him. When he looked up, he saw a shadowy figure on the steps. He was unable to describe the figure, but he was convinced that it was a man. He complained about the presence to a nearby theater staff member, who checked the staircase and found it empty. Strangely, the actor had no idea about the legends of the Lincoln, nor that the staircase was rumored to be haunted.

THE CEMETERY WHERE THE DEAD WALK

The beginnings of Greenwood Cemetery in Decatur are a mystery. There is no record to say when the first interments took place in the area of land that would someday be Greenwood. It was not the city's first official burial ground, but the Native Americans who lived here previously did use it for that purpose, as did the early settlers. The only trace they left behind was the large numbers of unmarked graves scattered about the present-day grounds.

In March 1857, the Greenwood Cemetery Association was organized, and the cemetery was incorporated into the city of Decatur. By 1900, Greenwood had become the most fashionable place in Decatur in which to be buried. It had also become quite popular as a recreational park, and noontime visitors often enjoyed their lunches on the grassy hills. Unfortunately, though, by the 1920s, the cemetery was broke and could no longer be maintained. It was allowed to revert to nature, and it wasn't long before it took the appearance of a forgotten graveyard, with overgrown brush, fallen branches, and tipped and broken gravestones. Hundreds of graves were left unattended and allowed to fall into disrepair. The stories and legends that would "haunt" Greenwood for years to come took root in the desolate conditions that existed in the oldest section of the graveyard. Tales of wandering spirits and glowing apparitions began to be told about the cemetery, and decay and decline came close to bringing about the destruction of the place. The cemetery became a forgotten spot in Decatur, remembered only as a spooky novelty.

In 1957, though, the city of Decatur took over ownership and operation of the cemetery. The city could not handle the cost of the restoration, so a number of organizations and private individuals volunteered to donate time and labor to save it. The restoration was largely a success, and despite a few setbacks, Greenwood Cemetery has managed to prosper over the years. Nevertheless, the place has not lost its eerie reputation, and the stories of ghosts and unexplained phenomena still mingle as fact and fiction blend with a strangeness unparalleled at any other location in the haunted heart of Illinois.

Nearly as many legends and strange stories have been told about Greenwood as there are people buried here—stories of the supernatural, of ghosts, phantoms, and things that go bump in the night. What follows is just a sampling of these eerie tales.

The story of the cemetery's most famous resident ghost, the Greenwood Bride, begins around 1930 and concerns a young couple that was engaged to be married. The young man was a reckless fellow and a bootlegger, and his future bride's family greatly disapproved of him. One summer night, the couple decided not to wait any longer to get married and made plans to elope. They would meet just after midnight, as soon as the young man could deliver one last shipment of whiskey and earn enough money for their wedding trip. But while delivering the bottles of whiskey, he was murdered. The killers, rival business-men, dumped his body into the Sangamon River, where two fishermen found it the next morning.

When his bride-to-be learned of his death, she went down to the river where his body had been found and, in a fit of grief, drowned herself. After the funeral, her body was laid to rest on a hill in Greenwood Cemetery. Her grieving parents buried their daughter in the wedding gown that she hadn't been able to wear. It has been said, however, that she does not rest there in peace. Over time, dozens of witnesses have reported seeing the Greenwood Bride—the ghost of a woman in a glowing bridal gown—weaving among the tombstones on that hill in the cemetery.

Could this sad young woman still be searching for the spirit of her murdered lover? No record remains as to where this man was laid to rest, so no one knows where his spirit may walk. Perhaps he is out there somewhere, still looking for the young woman that he was supposed to marry many years ago.

One of the cemetery's most enduring legends is the story behind the "ghost lights" that appear on the south side of the burial grounds. These small globes of light have been reported here for many decades and are still reported today. No logical reason exists for why they appear here, but the lore of the cemetery tells a strange and tragic story.

The legend tells of a flood that occurred many years ago, most likely between 1900 and 1905, and wiped out a portion of the cemetery. The Sangamon River, located just south of the cemetery, had been dammed in the late 1800s and was often prone to floods. During one particularly wet spring, the river overflowed its banks and washed into the lower sections of the cemetery. The surging water knocked over tombstones and even managed to wash graves away and force buried caskets to the surface. Many of them were carried downstream on the swollen river.

Once the water receded, it took many days to find the battered remains of the coffins, and many were never found at all. For some time after, farmers and fishermen were startled to find caskets, and even corpses, washing up on riverbanks some miles away. There were often questions as to the identities of the bodies, so many of them were buried again in unmarked and common graves. These new graves were placed on higher ground, up on the southern hills of Greenwood.

Since that time, it has been said, the mysterious lights have appeared on these hills—the spirits of those whose bodies washed away in the flood, wandering ghosts who are doomed to search forever for the place where their remains are now buried. Dozens of witnesses have claimed to see the "spook lights" on the hill, moving in and out among the old, weathered stones. The mystery of the lights has managed to elude all those who have attempted to solve it, but whether the cause is natural or supernatural, people still report seeing the lights along the edge of the graveyard today.

Located on a high, desolate hill in the far southwest corner of the cemetery is a section of the graveyard that is regarded today as Greenwood's most haunted spot. It was never intended for use, but it became a makeshift cemetery for prisoners during the Civil War.

At that time, a great many trains passed through Decatur. The city was on a direct line of the Illinois Central Railroad, which ran deep into the South. To the north, the line connected to a railroad that went to Chicago. Here it reached Camp Douglas, a prison for Confederates who were captured in battle. Many trains came north carrying these men, who were often sick and dying. Occasionally deceased soldiers were taken from the trains and buried in Greenwood Cemetery in unmarked graves.

One such prison train came through the city in 1863. The stories say that the train was filled with more than a hundred prisoners, many of whom had contracted yellow fever in the diseased swamps of the South.

The Union officers in charge of the train had attempted to separate the Confederates who had died in transit, but to no avail. Many of the other men were close to death from the infectious disease, and it was hard to tell which men were alive and which were not. The bodies were removed from the train and taken to Greenwood Cemetery, where they were unloaded and stacked at the base of a hill in the southwest corner of the graveyard. This location was possibly the least desirable spot in the cemetery. The hill was so steep that many of the grave diggers had trouble keeping their balance. It was the last place that anyone would want to be buried, and for this reason, it was perfect for the burials that took place.

The men hastily dug shallow graves and tossed the bodies of the Confederates inside. It has been said that without a doctor present, no one could have known just how many of the soldiers had actually died from yellow fever. Were all of those buried here really dead? Many say they were not, that some of them were accidentally buried alive, and this is why the area is the most haunted section of Greenwood.

Visitors who have come here, many of them knowing nothing about the bizarre history of this place, have told of hearing voices, strange sounds, footsteps in the grass, whispers, and cries of torment, and some even claim to have been touched or pushed by unseen hands. There are also accounts of the soldiers themselves returning from the other side of the grave. Over the years, visitors to the cemetery have reported seeing men in uniform walking among the tombstones—men that are strangely transparent.

ABRAHAM LINCOLN AND THE SPIRITUALISTS

No collection of the history and hauntings of Illinois would be complete without telling of the connections between Abraham Lincoln and the supernatural that were maintained throughout his life—and beyond. Much has been made of Lincoln's prophetic dreams and his belief in the spirit world, but why did those beliefs become such a prominent part of his life, and what event caused Lincoln to turn to contact with the dead?

A number of stories link President Lincoln to the supernatural. One of the most famous occurred when he was living in Springfield during the 1860 presidential elections. After winning the election, an exhausted Lincoln returned home and went into his bedroom for some much-needed rest. Near a couch where he lay down was a large bureau with a mirror on it, and Lincoln stared for a moment at his reflection in the glass. He then experienced what many would term a vision, which Lincoln later believed had prophetic meaning.

He saw that in the mirror, his face appeared to have two separate yet distinct images. The tip of one nose was about three inches away from the other one.

The vision vanished but appeared again a few moments later. It was clearer this time, and Lincoln realized that one of the faces was actually much paler than the other, almost with the coloring of death.

Later on that evening, he told his wife, Mary, of the strange vision, and she believed that she knew its significance. The healthy face was her husband's "real" face and indicated that he would serve his first term as president. The pale, ghostly image of the second face was a sign that he would be elected to a second term—but would not live to see its conclusion.

Lincoln's terms in office were defined by the Civil War, which took a terrible toll on the president, but there is no doubt that the most crippling blow he suffered in the White House was the death of his son Willie in 1862. Lincoln was sick at heart over Willie's death, and it was probably the most intense personal crisis in his life. Some historians have even called it the greatest blow he ever suffered. Even Confederate president Jefferson Davis expressed his condolences.

The cause of Willie's death remains a mystery, but it may have been an infection, or perhaps typhoid, caused by the unsanitary conditions in Washington, D.C., at the time. The onset of Willie's sickness occurred during the last days of January 1862. After playing in the snow with Tad, both of them developed a fever and a cold. Tad's illness soon passed, but Willie seemed to get worse. His parents kept him inside for a week and finally put him to bed. They summoned a doctor, who assured Mary that the boy would improve, despite the fact that Willie's lungs were congested and he was having trouble breathing.

One parent stayed with the frightened and sick boy at all times, and a nurse from one of the local hospitals came to help them. After a week of this, Mary had become too weak and exhausted to rise from her own bed, but Lincoln never left the boy's side, sleeping and eating in a chair next to his bed. As Willie grew worse, the doctors lost hope for the child. Soon his mind wandered and he failed to recognize anyone, including his beloved father. Death came for Willie on the afternoon of February 20, 1862.

The funeral was held in the East Room at the White House. The service was short. Willie had been embalmed to make the trip back to Springfield and be buried beside his brother, but Lincoln changed his mind about that at the last minute. He accepted an offer made to him by a friend, William Thomas Carroll, to place the body of Willie in one of the crypts in the Carroll family tomb. This would be until Lincoln retired from the presidency and returned to live in Springfield. He could not bear the idea of having Willie so far away from him just yet.

In fact, Lincoln returned to the cemetery the next day to watch the body as it was moved from the cemetery chapel to the crypt. The tomb was built into the side of a hill in a remote area of the cemetery. It was a beautiful and peaceful spot, but Lincoln wasn't able to leave his son unattended there for long.

Word got out that Lincoln returned to the tomb on two occasions and had Willie's coffin opened. The doctor had embalmed Willie so perfectly that everyone said he seemed to be only sleeping. Lincoln claimed that he felt compelled to look upon his boy's face just one last time.

After the funeral, Lincoln tried to go on about his work, but his spirit had been crushed by Willie's death. One week after the funeral, he closed himself up in his office all day and wept. It has often been said that Lincoln was on the verge of suicide at this point, but none can say for sure. He did withdraw even further into himself, though, and he began to look more closely at the spiritual matters that had interested him for so long.

Although many Lincoln scholars say otherwise, it is more than possible that Abraham Lincoln didn't just believe in the supernatural, but he actually participated in it. There are others who say that he actually attended séances that were held in the White House. Whether he accepted the movement or not, it is a fact that many Spiritualists were often guests there. Several of them were even said to have given him warnings about the dark shadows that hung over his life.

While Lincoln avoided the Spiritualists in public, Mary embraced them openly. She had been quick to turn to contact with the other side for comfort after Willie's death. Once he was gone, Mary never again entered the White House guest room where he died, or the room in which the funeral viewing was held. Some historians claim that this was the beginning of Mary's mental instability—not because of the mediums, but because of her fervent grief. The obsession over Spiritualism was just one of the symptoms, they believe, while her headaches, mood swings, and bursts of irrational temper were growing worse.

Mary began meeting with a number of different Spiritualists and invited many to the White House, as each claimed to be able to "lift the thin veil" and allow Mary to communicate with Willie. Mary's closest Spiritualist companion was Nettie Colburn Maynard, with whom there is some record that Lincoln also met. A familiar tale is often told about a séance held by Nettie Maynard in 1863, where a grand piano levitated off the floor while the medium was playing the instrument. Lincoln and Colonel Simon Kase were present, and it is said that both men climbed onto the piano, only to have it jump and shake so hard that they climbed down. It is recorded that Lincoln later referred to the levitation as proof of an invisible power.

Rumors spread that Lincoln had an interest in the spirit world. In England, a piece of sheet music was published that portrayed him holding a candle while violins and tambourines flew about his head. The piece of music was called "The Dark Séance Polka," and the caption below the illustration of the president read, "Abraham Lincoln and the Spiritualists."

Perhaps the most famous supernatural incident connected to Lincoln was his last prophetic dream of his assassination. Years later, Ward Hill Lamon, a close friend of Lincoln, remembered that the president had continued to be haunted by the strange vision that he experienced in the mirror in 1860. Several years after that, shortly before his assassination, Lincoln recounted an eerie dream of death to Lamon and Mary. In the dream, he walked through the darkened White House and heard many voices weeping in despair. He eventually arrived in the East Room, where a casket was on display. He asked a soldier that was standing guard who had died in the White House.

The guard replied: "The President. He was killed by an assassin."

Lincoln was murdered just a few days later, and his body was displayed in the East Room of the White House. Mary recalled this dream of her husband's quite vividly in the days that followed. It was said that her first coherent word after the assassination was a muttered statement about his dream being prophetic.

THE GHOST WHO WOULDN'T LEAVE THE LAKE CLUB

The Lake Club in Springfield opened as a nightclub in 1940, but the building on Fox Bridge Road had seen many incarnations in the years prior to that, including as several restaurants and even a skating rink called the Joy Inn. Then two dance promoters, Harold Henderson and Hugo Giovagnoli, renovated the place and opened it for business.

The club soon became one of the hottest night spots in Illinois, drawing customers from all over the state. It boasted a raised dance floor surrounded by a railing, curved walls, and a swanky atmosphere that made patrons feel as though a New York club had been transported to the shores of Lake Springfield. The owners concentrated on bringing big-name entertainment to the club and succeeded. Among the many top performers were Bob Hope, Ella Fitzgerald, Guy Lombardo, Pearl Bailey, Spike Jones, Nelson Eddy, Woody Herman, and Mickey Rooney. The constant stream of entertainers and big bands drew capacity crowds to the club every night.

The Lake Club thrived for nearly two decades, becoming known not only for its swinging entertainment, but also for its first-rate gambling. Wealthy customers and the society elite of Springfield and Decatur frequented the club for the musical guests as well as the billiard tables, craps and gaming tables, slot machines, and card games. This part of the club operated in secret in a back part of the building, known only to high rollers and special customers. In December 1958, however, the golden days of the Lake Club came to an end. The partners had survived many setbacks over the years, from lawsuits to foreclosures, but the club could not survive two undercover detectives who gained access to the gambling rooms that Christmas season.

The club was immediately shut down, although the restaurant and dance hall were allowed to operate. This was not enough to save the business. Things began to falter in the wake of the raid, and the club finally closed down in the 1960s. Hugo Giovagnoli refused to give up on the Lake Club and opened it up again in the 1970s, with other parties managing different projects in the building. During this time in the club's history, it was managed by Bill Carmean and Tom Blasko as a rock club. In 1980, it was leased by Pat Tavine, who also operated it as a rock club until 1988, when it closed down for good. Sadly, the building was destroyed by fire in 1992.

It was in August 1979 that the Lake Club, which soon became known as the Sober Duck Rock and Disco Club, gained national notoriety. It was at this time when the ghost of Albert "Rudy" Cranor was finally put to rest.

According to the many patrons and staff members who had experiences there, the haunting of the Lake Club first began in 1974. At the time, the club was in the midst of a revival in interest, and the business was under the ownership of Blasko and Carmean, two Springfield men who were booking rock acts into the club.

People started reporting odd sounds in the building, as well as a feeling of being watched in some of the rooms. A piano played by itself. Lights turned on and off, doors opened and closed, and things moved about by themselves. By 1976, the haunting had intensified, and things began happening more often and in front of more witnesses.

Bill Carmean was the first of the club's staff to guess the identity of the ghost who was plaguing the establishment. He recalled that a former employee had committed suicide in the building several years before. On a lark, he started calling the ghost by this man's name—Rudy.

Albert "Rudy" Cranor had worked as a bartender at the Lake Club during its heyday in the 1950s. He was always described as being well liked and popular with the entertainers and the customers. A very large man, well over 250 pounds, with snow white hair, he was remembered as one of the club's most memorable characters.

After the club fell on hard times following the gambling raid, Rudy also started experiencing some personal difficulties. He was a very private person, so no one really knew what was going on, but they did notice that he began to drink heavily while on the job. He also seemed to be more tired than usual, and dark circles appeared under his eyes. One night, he got so sick that he had to be rushed to the hospital. He returned to the club after a two-week stay in the hospital, but he was never the same again.

On June 27, 1968, Rudy committed suicide with a high-powered rifle in one of the back rooms at the club. No one was ever sure why Rudy had killed himself, but apparently he didn't stay gone for long, returning in a few short years to haunt his beloved club.

The strange events at the club continued in the form of weird antics and pranks believed to be carried out by the ghost of Rudy Cranor. A frightening event took place in the summer of 1979, when a waitress at the club claimed to see the floating head of a man with white hair who warned that one of the owners of the club was going to die. The waitress fled the room in hysterics, and Tom Blasko stated that when he went to investigate, he found that the room was ice cold.

Blasko and Carmean were unnerved by the ghost's warning. The two men waited for something terrible to happen, and then, two weeks after the incident, Harold Henderson, one of the original owners of the club, died at the age of sixty-nine. He was still the owner of the building itself and was an owner that Rudy would have known during his lifetime.

Blasko was shaken by the incident, and after two weeks of living in fear, he decided to try to get rid of the ghost. He contacted his parish priest, but the man declined to get involved. The priest suggested that Blasko pray for Rudy on his own, and Tom spent the next six months carrying a rosary around the club with him, but it didn't help—Rudy was still there.

Finally, in August 1979, Blasko attended a high school class reunion and ran into one of his former classmates, the Reverend Gary Dilley, a priest who now lived in Texas. Tom mentioned the problems at the club to Father Dilley, who was intrigued. After some discussion, he agreed to come out to the club and take a look around. After arriving at the club, Father Dilley also sensed something out of the ordinary there. He was convinced that something was going on, but he declined to do an exorcism of the club. To do that, the case would require a thorough investigation and permission from the local bishop, which he doubted he would get. Instead, he decided to bless the place and pray there, hoping this would perhaps put Rudy's spirit to rest.

He contacted two other priests, and together they blessed the building with holy water and prayed for the soul of Rudy Cranor. Eventually they entered the room in which he had committed suicide and prayed that his spirit would be at rest.

So was that the end of the haunting? Apparently it was. The same people who had considered the club to be haunted were now sure that Rudy had departed. The day of the religious ceremony was the last day anyone was aware of Rudy's presence in the building. It seems that the prayers and blessings helped the bartender find his way to the other side. Perhaps the intervention of the priests was all he needed to be persuaded to move on. Rudy had finally found some peace.

THE LEGENDS OF VOORHIES CASTLE

Located on a lonely stretch of highway in eastern Central Illinois is an isolated village called Voorhies. Very little is left of the town these days, save for a few houses, an abandoned church—and the haunted Voorhies Castle.

The legends about this rambling old mansion have been some of the most often repeated tales in the region, and the chilling stories have not been forgotten. Just a few short years ago, Voorhies Castle was still a place of legends. The dark tales concerning its shadowed beginnings and haunted past had been recounted by generation after generation. The place became the perfect model for a haunted house on the prairie.

The story of Voorhies Castle began in 1867, with the arrival of a Swedish immigrant named Nels Larson. He settled near Galesburg and went to work for a local farmer, soon earning a reputation as a hard and efficient worker. Larson saved every dollar he made, and within a short time, he moved south and settled in Piatt County, near the town of Bement. Here he went to work for a local farmer and landowner named William Voorhies.

Nels Larson started out with little, but he was an ambitious man. He went into debt to buy some teams of horses and eventually borrowed money to purchase his own property. In 1872, Larson sent for his fiancée, Johannah Nilson, from Sweden, and they were married later that same year.

Nels continued to buy more land and lease other parcels. He also had a number of farmers working for him, renting his property in exchange for a portion of the proceeds from the harvest. In addition to his own farm, he was a partial owner in many others. The small town of Voorhies, which Larson now owned, was also growing, consisting mostly of small businesses and tenant homes rented by his farmers. It had a church, general store, barbershop, jeweler, blacksmith, and postmaster, as well as a grain elevator, corn crib, and several barns. The post office was granted a license for the sale of postal money orders, and locals could purchase tickets for travel on the Wabash Railroad line, which passed through town. The rail station was also useful for the loading and unloading of grain and cattle. The grain elevator was added to the town in 1897 and was operated by Larson's son George, who was also the postmaster.

By 1900, Larson was firmly entrenched as the "ruler" of his vast domain. He had lived in several houses around the area but now decided that he needed a manor house from which to oversee his property. This house, later dubbed Voorhies Castle, would be patterned after a chalet in his native Sweden. Larson contacted a Chicago architect to draw up plans to his specifications. He then hired a contractor, and construction began that summer.

The house was a strange mixture of styles and eccentricities. It was fitted with twin towers on the front of the structure, huge doors, and abnormally large windows for the time. Inside the house was a large reception hall with an oak fireplace. Larson had brought an artist from Sweden especially for the purpose of hand-carving this fireplace and two others in the house. Each doorway had sliding doors leading to the adjoining rooms.

The west parlor contained a cherry wood fireplace. This parlor led into the west tower, and its doorway was adorned with wooden scrollwork. The ceiling was papered and decorated with clouds and stars. It was in this room that Larson conducted most of his business affairs.

On the opposite side of the reception hall was the east parlor. This room was more designed for lady visitors, with emerald furniture, scrolled doorways, a bookcase secretary, and even a fainting couch for the lady whose corset stays might be too tight. The walls in this room were not papered, but covered with a smooth, slack lime plaster.

The house boasted indoor plumbing, and a bathroom with all the latest innovations was located between the east parlor and the back room, which served as Johannah's sewing room and an extra bedroom.

The dining room was also located on the first floor and boasted a beautiful parquet floor designed of maple, mahogany, birch, oak, and sycamore pieces. It featured a marble-topped sideboard and a dining-room table that could be extended to seat twenty-four people. In the corner of the room was a gold couch where Larson napped each day following his lunch. A telephone and doorbell, both battery-operated devices, were mounted on the wall of the dining room.

The kitchen was small but filled to capacity. It had a tiled floor and contained a drop-leaf table and chairs, high cupboard, stove, sink, and water heater. The kitchen was further cramped by five doors that exited off it, leading to the basement, upstairs, back porch, dining room, and a small pantry that was lined from floor to ceiling with shelves and cupboards.

Floral carpeting climbed the stairs and extended into the bedrooms. The largest of the upstairs chambers was the master bedroom, which extended across the east end of the house. It was dominated by a huge rosewood bed and dresser that had to be moved into position before the house could be completed. The tower room adjacent to this bedroom offered the best view of the land, and it has been said that Larson looked out over his holdings every morning when he rose from bed.

The running water in the house was provided by 2,000-gallon wooden cisterns in which water was stored and forced by compressed air into the kitchen and bathroom. A steel, airtight tank received the water from the cisterns by hand pump. The water compressed the air already in the tank, and then forced the water upstairs. Five minutes of pumping would supply the household with enough water for the entire day. A hot-water heater in the kitchen provided heated rainwater, used for cooking and drinking. There was also an auxiliary water system that used rainwater for the fountains located in the twin flower beds in the front yard.

The other side of the basement contained a coal bin and a hot-air furnace that sent air into all the rooms of the house. A battery-operated thermostat controlled the temperature. The house was never equipped with an electrical system during the period when the Larson family lived here.

Only the finest materials were used in the construction of the house, delaying its completion until 1904. On many occasions, Larson returned entire loads of lumber to the warehouse after discovering a few boards with knots in them. The total cost of the castle was around $9,000.

The most eccentric addition to the estate was a large barn with a clock tower on it, which Nels insisted should be included on the property. The stories say that Larson had a fascination, or perhaps obsession, with clocks. They could be found all over the house, from a large grandfather clock in the reception area to small timepieces scattered on top of the wooden trunk in his bedroom. One day in 1905, Nels decided he wanted to install a large clock in his barn. He ordered a Seth Thomas clock from a jeweler in Monticello and began construction on the new building. The barn took almost five years to complete, even longer than it took to build the house, and was not finished until 1910. The new structure had to be equipped with a sixty-eight-foot-tall tower and given enough support that it could hold the nearly two-ton clock mechanism.

Legend states that the clock mysteriously struck thirteen times at the moment of Nels Larson's death in 1923, as though the man and machine were somehow connected. The stories go on to say that the clock continued this odd activity for five decades, ringing out on the anniversary of its owner's passing. The clock tower remained an odd landmark on the prairie until the summer of 1976, when it was destroyed by a tornado. It has been said that the now phantom clock continues to chime each March 29, at the very hour that Nels Larson passed from this world to the next.

The Larson family resided in the house for a number of years. The most mysterious event during their occupancy occurred in 1914, when Johannah died.

Many have speculated that she had a heart attack on the staircase, but the real cause of her death remains a mystery to this day. One of the field hands had gone to the house one afternoon to find her lying in a crumpled heap on the floor. Nels was so stunned by this event that he left the house that night and went to his daughter's home in Cerro Gordo, never to return. He left behind all of the furniture and even his clothing and personal belongings.

The house was completely abandoned. For years it seemed trapped in time, with clothing in the closets, the table still set for dinner, Johannah's apron hanging over the back of a chair, and even food still sitting on the cold stove.

Johannah was gone—but did she ever really leave the house, even after death? Legend has it that on certain nights, an eerie light could be seen coming from the east tower of the house. Those who were brave enough to venture onto the property claimed to see Johannah framed in the window of the room.

Nels Larson died in 1923, and his will specified that the house should remain in the family. But none of them wanted to live in a house without electricity, so it was left to decay, remembered only by time and the elements.

Another strange tale was linked to the death of Nels Larson. According to this story, his body was returned to the castle to lie in state before the funeral. The casket was placed in the reception hall near the window, with a basket of flowers at its head. When the basket was removed after the funeral, a hole was said to have appeared in the carpet where it had been resting. Dozens of witnesses saw the mysterious hole later, but exactly how it got there was shrouded in mystery.

Over the years, a number of tenants moved into the house, but none stayed for long. It's likely that they were chased away by the deteriorating conditions of the house more so than by the ghosts. But the rapid succession of tenants and the spooky atmosphere of the place combined to give the castle a ghostly reputation, and the tales surrounding it grew and became more elaborate as the years went by. It was said that someone died of fright in the house and the imprint of his or her body was still pressed into a couch in the living room. According to another story, a pillar in the west parlor that once held a large fern would inexplicably spin around under its own power, and it spun so much that it eventually wore down into a circular area on the floor.

In 1967, the grandchildren of Nels Larson donated the castle to the Illinois Pioneer Heritage Center in Monticello. The center opened the house as a tourist attraction, reportedly drawing up to 30,000 visitors each year who came both to view the unique architecture of the place and to soak up some of the ghostly ambience. The house was simply too expensive to take care of, however, and it was closed down once again.

Only caretakers remained to watch over the place. Many of them claimed that the lights in the house refused to stay off and that windows would open on their own. One of them also said that often after he had closed up the house, turned off the lights, and made sure all the windows were closed and locked, by the time he got outside to his car, the lights would be on again and several of the windows would have slipped open.

The notoriety of the house began to fade by the mid-1970s. It was eventually sold, but over the course of the next few years, it was frequently vacant and began to deteriorate again. The decay of the mansion became the biggest problem that all the new owners and tenants faced, along with fending off the sightseers for whom the ghostly landmark was still an attraction. Within the last few years, though, the current owners of the house have finally been able to revitalize the place and restore it to its former glory.

Whether the ghosts remain here is unknown, but the legends of Voorhies Castle have simply never faded away.

THE TRAGEDY OF TOWANDA MEADOWS

Every one of us who has traveled along the interstate north of Bloomington, Illinois, has seen the house, nestled eerily in the cornfields just off in the distance, and every one of us with an interest in old houses and haunted history has wondered about it. The brick Italianate mansion seems out of place on the Illinois prairie, looking mournfully toward a highway and a railroad line that seems to have passed it by, leaving it stranded in the distant past. It crumbled there for many years—lost, abandoned, seemingly forgotten, and some say, haunted by tragedies of yesterday. It is a house of unrealized dreams, great fortune, and premature death, but is strangely suited to the shadowy corners of Central Illinois.

The grand house, which came to be known as Towanda Meadows, was built in 1874–1875 by William R. Duncan, a pioneer farmer and stock-raiser who came to Illinois in 1863. When he erected the mansion, it was said that he purposely set out to make it so impressive that it would be noticed by travelers between St. Louis and Chicago. He attained his objective, building an Italianate mansion with six fireplaces, a winding staircase with hard-carved walnut spindles, and walls that were more than a foot thick. But he was destined to only enjoy the house for a short time. Not long after it was completed, death and tragedy came calling.

But William had already known his share of tragedy. He was born in Kentucky in December 1818. His parents were wealthy, and William inherited his father's estate when he was only eighteen. By that time, he had already lost his mother and one of his sisters, Sally, had been declared insane.

William married his first wife, Nancy Redmon, in 1835. She died a dozen years later, and he married again, this time to Mary Chorn Quisenberry, and they would have four children, Nannie, Henry, James, and Mary Elizabeth.

At the height of the Civil War, in October 1863, William, a Union supporter and abolitionist, decided to move from his family from Kentucky to Illinois. They traveled by train and ended up in Towanda, north of Bloomington, where they rented a house until a new home could be built. But the start of the family's happy life in Illinois was shattered by the death of Mary Duncan on February 23, 1864. William was devastated by the loss of another beloved wife and the children were heartbroken, especially Mary Elizabeth, who was only three-years-old at the time.

Late in 1864, William, now only forty-five and widowed twice, traveled back to Kentucky and married his third wife, Sarah Ann Bean. The newlyweds returned to Illinois and William began building a cattle business and amassing a fortune. He became respected in the region for his expertise in farming and cattle raising and introduced some of the finest breeds of foreign cattle to the area.

Tragedy visited the Duncan family again on June 16, 1868, when Henry, age twelve, drowned in a pond on the family's property. During his son's funeral, a grieving William had the grave of his second wife, Mary, opened up so that he could say goodbye to her one last time.

A few years later, construction was started on Duncan's three-story mansion, Towanda Meadows. The house was unlike anything that had been seen in the area before, and locals came from far and wide to watch the construction take place and to marvel at the unusual elements of the house.

Towanda Meadows was completed in 1875 but, sadly, William lived in the house for less than a year before he died in October 1876 at the age of only fifty-seven. At the time of his death, he was returning home from the State Fair, which was held in Ottawa, Illinois, that fall. He had been depressed for some time, following the death of his last remaining sister, Elizabeth, who had died in Clinton a short time before. Many blamed his melancholy for the fact that he was unable to shake off a severe cold that he contracted at the fair. After becoming ill in Ottawa, he was put to bed at the home of his friend Abner Strawn and remained there for several days. Feeling better, he departed for Towanda, but only made it as far as Normal before he collapsed. He was taken to the home of relatives and died Sarah by his side.

Sarah remained at the farm for a time with eight children, five of her own and three of William and Mary's. They had little time to mourn as drama, tragedy, and death continued to plague the family.

Nannie, William's oldest daughter with his wife Mary, had become a schoolteacher and married Franklin Barnes, a successful farmer, in 1878. They had a daughter, Lucy, who was born in 1880. In 1884, Nannie contracted tuberculosis. Franklin sold his farm and moved his wife and daughter to Pomona, California. He hoped that the mild climate might make her better. Unfortunately, California did not turn out to be beneficial for Nannie. She continued to decline and as she neared death, she told her husband that she wanted to return to Illinois to live out her final days. She passed away while they were on their way home.

Tragedy struck the family again in 1896 when Nannie's daughter, Lucy, also died from tuberculosis on the day before her sixteenth birthday.

William and Mary's third child, James, was only eighteen when his father died in 1876. Nelson Jones was appointed by the court as his guardian and James lived each winter in Texas, where he raised horses and brought them back to Illinois for sale. In September 1878, James married Flora Dillon and they had a son, Levi. James worked hard to improve the farm, importing horses from overseas, and becoming prosperous. A second son, Floyd, was born in November 1882.

But James and his family couldn't escape tragedy. In 1883, James, Flora, Flora's sister, Ida Dillon Harding, and other members of the Dillon family, traveled to France. James planned to arrange the purchase of several horses and see the sights with his family. As they were preparing to make their way back across the Atlantic, Ida became seriously ill and died.

Her death was just the beginning. In just three years, James went from a prominent businessman to a severely depressed and mentally ill young man. His malady struck in his late twenties and was likely an onset of bipolar disorder, for which no diagnosis existed at the time. In 1886, he was sent to an insane asylum for five years. While he was away, his money largely disappeared and accusations of theft were made against his son, Levi. He was released from the hospital in 1891 and he and Flora divorced. After that, he vanished from history.

Mary Elizabeth, Mary and William's youngest child, married Ellis Dillon, Flora's brother, in 1883. The couple later moved to Wisconsin and Ellis enrolled at the University of Madison for training to become an electrical engineer. They were happy for years but then in September 1918, Mary was granted a divorce from her husband on the grounds of cruel and inhuman treatment. According to her testimony, Ellis simply stopped speaking to her one day. This went on for five years. She was unable to cite a cause for this treatment. Ellis later moved to Montana, but what became of Mary Elizabeth is a mystery.

After William's death, Sarah and her five children with William remained at Towanda Meadows for a short time before returning to Kentucky. Sarah eventually died of pneumonia in February 1922 at the age of eighty-six. She never remarried.

Towanda Meadows was sold and went through a succession of owners. During the twentieth century, tenants occupied the grand old home. The fireplaces were bricked up, the second and third story windows shuttered, and the house was allowed to decline.

It was the tenants who lived in the house who told strange tales of ghosts and lingering memories. Many of them spoke of footsteps on the stairs and in the hallways, whispers, sounds of a woman weeping, and knocking at the front door during the wee hours of the night. Every one of these weird happenings can be directly tied to the mansion's tragic past with a woman crying for a lost child and the fateful knock that summoned Sarah to the bedside of her dying husband. History has left an impression on this creaking old place and seems to be replaying itself over and over again.

A former resident of the house once related his own encounter with a spectral woman on the second floor. He was only a boy at the time but clearly remembered exploring the upper floors of the house when he was living there with his family. In one of the closed-off bedrooms, he saw a woman standing and gazing out of the window. When he sharply inhaled at the sight, the woman quickly turned around and then vanished in front of his eyes. He never forgot the incident, but who the woman might have been is unknown. Despite the efforts of local researchers, no Duncan family photographs have ever turned up.

Do phantoms still linger at Towanda Meadows? It seems they do. A young couple purchased the house in the mid-2010s and have been working to restore it to its former glory. They have not been immune to the strange, unexplained sounds that others have experienced there in the past.

ILLINOIS RIVER VALLEY

One of the most beautiful areas of the Prairie State is the land in the northern portion that follows the Illinois River. It is a region of great history and often eerie beauty that has connections to the earliest days of the territory. It was here where Indian massacres took place, French explorers settled, and a great many ghosts seem to have been left behind.

SPIRITS OF STARVED ROCK

Starved Rock, located near Utica, is regarded as one of the state's greatest natural wonders. Long before it gained its infamous name, the huge outcropping was the site of Fort St. Louis, a sanctuary constructed by the famous French explorer Sieur de La Salle and his adventurous companion, Henri de Tonty. The rock rose more than 120 feet from the currents of the Illinois River below and offered only sandstone cliffs and shadowy crevices as ways of obtaining the summit. Here the French established an outpost and traded goods like hatchets, traps, kettles, and blankets with the Indians for buffalo and beaver skins.

As Fort St. Louis grew atop the towering rock in 1683, Tonty and La Salle roamed the region. The Indians brought furs to the rock, and the pelts were stored in new warehouses. The settlement grew, and soon more than 20,000 Native Americans were living and trading near the fort. The tribes gathered here were at peace, and it looked as though La Salle's commercial enterprise would be a great success. But a political setback caused La Salle to lose his support in France, and his supplies from the north were cut off. He left Fort St. Louis and began to seek out a new trade route to the south, journeying down the Illinois River to the Mississippi.

Henri de Tonty stayed behind at the rock, and for ten years, between two dangerous journeys, the fort remained his home. Here he counseled with the chiefs, sent agents to outlying tribes, and conducted trade with Canada. Tonty was by turns an Indian fighter, a diplomat, a businessman, and an independent frontiersman operating with only frail lines of communication in a rough region that was larger than all of France. He survived attacks by the rampaging Iroquois as well as political and financial attacks by jealous rivals. When he learned that his friend La Salle had vanished while exploring the regions along the southern part of the Mississippi, Tonty went in search of him. Two years passed before he learned La Salle's fate—the explorer had been killed by his own rebellious men and his bones picked clean by wolves in Texas. Weary from his journey and wasted by fever, Tonty returned to Fort St. Louis in September 1690.

By the following year, the decade of trading at the fort had badly depleted the game in the region, so Tonty moved his headquarters to Lake Peoria. More political problems eventually drove him out of the region, and he traveled south to Mobile, Alabama. He died of disease in September 1704 and was buried far from the Illinois country that he had so bravely conquered. Or was he?

According to some of the Native Americans who knew and respected the explorer, Tonty returned to the rock to die—many years after his reported death at Mobile. They said that he came as a white-haired old man with a staff in his hand, groping his way along the twisting path to the summit. It became a local belief that the spirit of Tonty still haunts the rock on nights when the moon appears over the river and silvers the wild and vanished country that he once knew.

After Tonty's departure, the fort was abandoned and fell into ruin. Within a few years, though, the rock became the scene of death and tragedy and finally earned the name by which it is known today.

Long before the French explorers came to the region, it was inhabited by Native American hunters and wanderers. They were the sole occupants of the land, with their small villages scattered across the prairie and nestled close to the rivers and water sources.

When the French encountered these Indians at the mouth of the Des Moines River, they called themselves the Illiniwek, which actually translated to mean "the men." This designation was intended to separate them from the Iroquois, who were their mortal enemies and whom they referred to as "animals." From that time on, they became known as the Illinois Confederation, and it was from this band that the state later took its name. The confederation was made up of several tribes who had banded together for the purpose of defense. They held a large portion of the state, which they shared with several other tribes, including the powerful Kickapoo.

In the late 1600s, the Illiniwek were nearly wiped out by the rampaging Iroquois and Fox Indians, and their numbers grew smaller. They were constantly beaten and harassed by their enemies, and the arrival of the white settlers ruined their hunting grounds, bringing the Illiniwek occupation to an end.

Prior to that, the Illiniwek battled courageously against the attacks from the other tribes. The Fox in particular had staged a series of bloody skirmishes against the Illiniwek. By the last months of 1721, the fighting between them had grown so intense that the Fox allied with other tribes and pursued the struggling Illiniwek to the Illinois River. They sought safety atop the same rock where La Salle and Tonty had constructed Fort St. Louis years before. At first the fortress seemed a safe refuge from the Fox, Winnebago, and Sauk tribes below, but the Illiniwek soon realized they were trapped—there was no way to escape from the rock. Their enemy waited below, and behind them was a steep drop to the rocky banks and swirling waters of the Illinois River.

The Illiniwek began to slowly waste away from sickness, cold, and especially hunger. Most of those who tried to escape were killed after jumping from the edge of the cliff. A few of the more daring warriors attempted to flee through the forest, only to be struck down and slaughtered by those who were laying siege below. Others who were captured were horrifically burned at the stake.

No one really knows how long the Illiniwek were trapped on the summit that came to be known as Starved Rock. A number of accounts say that at least a dozen of them escaped through the woods or by the river and took shelter with friendly tribes or French trappers. Other stories tell of miraculous escapes and a mysterious snow that fell one night and covered the tracks of the desperate Illiniwek, giving them just enough time to escape. When they were gone, they left nothing behind at the old fort save for items they could not carry and the bodies of the dead.

By the end of the ordeal, the once great Illinois Confederation had collapsed to less than a hundred persons. Eventually they were all sent to a reservation in Kansas. It is believed that not a single descendant of the Illiniwek nation lives today. They were completely wiped out by the events at Starved Rock and vanished forever—or did they?

According to legend, spirits of some of the desperate Illiniwek still roam the woods near the base of Starved Rock. The ghosts of those who died while trying to escape have lingered here, and the sounds of cries and screams are sometimes heard in the forest. Starved Rock is a place where history has left a very dark and indelible impression indeed.

HAUNTED HOTEL KASKASKIA

Built in 1915 by the architects of the luxurious Drake and Blackstone Hotels in Chicago, the Kaskaskia in LaSalle was meant to be a big-city hotel in a small town. It was constructed at a time when LaSalle was on the verge of becoming a major manufacturing town for cement and zinc. It was also home to Westclox, one of America's leading timepiece companies in the early 1900s. The plans for the hotel were so grand that they required fifty-four investors to bring the project to fruition.

Once it was completed, the hotel was considered to be a showplace of the Illinois Valley region. It attracted customers from Chicago and all over the Midwest and played host to lavish parties, receptions, weddings, and more. The hotel enjoyed great success for many years, but eventually, without the manufacturing base to support business, it fell on hard times and closed down. Plans are currently under way to restore the hotel and reopen it in the future. Over the years, staff members and guests have complained about phantom voices, eerie sounds, and doors that open and close without assistance. In the lobby of the building, many have reported an unusual phenomenon—coins that just appear without explanation. They can often be found lying on the floor, and where they come from, no one seems to know. Witnesses have sometimes stated that they heard the eerie clink of the coins as they dropped from the ether.

Elevators in the hotel have a habit of behaving very strangely. They tend to travel to floors where no one is found, and the staff elevator would take employees to floors that they hadn't pushed the buttons to reach, especially the basement.

The most famous ghost of the Kaskaskia is that of a young woman who plunged to her death from the sixth-story ballroom in the late 1940s. At one end of the room was a balcony that offered a full view of the surrounding area and of Wright Street below. No one knows just what happened to cause this woman to fall. The official story was suicide, but rumors have swirled for decades that she may have been murdered.

Regardless of how she died, it seems that she has haunted the ballroom ever since. Staff members and guests have reported hearing the sound of her dance shoes clicking across the floor throughout the day and night. On many occasions, guests on the fifth floor have heard music playing and someone walking around in the ballroom above them. A check of the room has always revealed a locked and abandoned ballroom, and the staff simply dismissed the sounds as one last dancer, still looking for her partner after all these years.

THE IRRITATED GHOST OF THE NINTH STREET PUB

The Ninth Street Pub in LaSalle has been a popular restaurant and tavern since the late 1960s. In the early days, the pub was located right next door to the home of an elderly woman named Mrs. Sonnenburg. Although she liked the proprietor of the tavern, John Ebener, she hated the fact that the noisy tavern, with its rowdy crowds and live music, was located so close to her home. She constantly, although good-naturedly, harassed John about this for years, until she passed away one day in the mid-1970s.

Mrs. Sonnenburg died under very mysterious circumstances, which still have not been fully explained to this day. Her body was not discovered for several days after her death, and when she was found, having passed away from a stroke, she was locked inside her bedroom closest. It has been surmised that perhaps she was getting something out of the closet, suffered the stroke, and then collapsed into the closet, somehow locking the door behind her.

John Ebener later purchased the small house next door to the pub, knocked down some walls, and incorporated it into the tavern. The house thus became a part of the pub, including the closet where Mrs. Sonnenburg died, which is next to the restrooms today. Pool tables were installed, and the pub managed to more than double its size. Soon after the work was finished, the staff began to realize that strange things were taking place in the bar—mostly in the section that had been the old house. Lights began turning on and off by themselves, doors opened and closed, and footsteps were often heard, even when no one else was present. Customers and staff members have often complained of feeling as if they have been touched or had their hair or clothing tugged on in that part of the tavern, as if someone were trying to get their attention.

One day, a brand new bartender, who knew nothing about the tavern or that it was alleged to be haunted, walked into the side of the bar near the pool tables and was chilled to hear the disembodied voice of an old woman asking, "What the hell are you doing here?" The bartender turned to see who was there and found the place empty. It seems that Mrs. Sonnenburg is still protective about her home, even from beyond the grave.

THE SPRING VALLEY VAMPIRE AND THE HATCHET MAN

One of the strangest tales of the Illinois River Valley is undoubtedly that of the spectral vampire that has been said to linger in Spring Valley's Old Lithuanian Cemetery for many years. Stories have been told of a shadowy figure in black clothing who haunts this graveyard, lurking about on the grounds and often preying on local pets. Many witnesses claim that they have found slaughtered dogs and cats, always drained of blood, in the cemetery, especially around the old Massock Mausoleum.

The mausoleum is the final resting place of the Massock brothers, who were once well-known butchers in the city. The Massock home was located a short distance away from the burial ground and gave rise to its own legend, that of the Hatchet Man. This ominous figure is still believed by some to hide in the ruins of the old mansion, waiting for unsuspecting victims with his ax. Legend has it that this phantom figure is the ghost of the Massock estate's old care-taker, who murdered his wife—with an ax, of course—back in the 1920s.

It is said that the Massock Mausoleum is the home of the cemetery vampire, who emerges from this crypt. In 1967, two local teenagers broke into the tomb and stole the head from one of the corpses entombed there. The boys were later caught and punished, but the vandalism did nothing to dispel the stories, and incidents and sightings continued in the graveyard for years.

One night in the early 1980s, a hardened Vietnam veteran went out to the cemetery with several friends to see if the stories of the creature were true. As they trudged across the grounds toward the tomb, they were startled by a move-ment from out of the shadows. Suddenly, what they described as a gaunt, pale figure that seemed to radiate evil lurched toward them. The veteran, who had brought a handgun with him on the outing, pulled out the gun and reportedly shot the creature five times at point-blank range. To his amazement, the bullets had no effect. Angry now, the figure came toward the group, and they ran from the cemetery in a panic.

Not long after, researchers from Chicago heard about the incident and decided to come to Spring Valley and investigate the cemetery. The group arrived one afternoon about a month after the earlier party had allegedly encountered the strange creature and set out across the grounds in search of the crypt. When they found it, they rapped on the door, but not surprisingly, they received no response. They then poked a wooden rod into a small vent on the side, and when they did, something black and wormy shot out from the hole and twisted onto the ground. Unnerved, the investigators took off running.

Later that afternoon, though, they gathered their wits and returned to the cemetery around dusk, bringing with them a bottle of holy water, which they

　　　　　HAUNTED ILLINOIS

emptied into the vent. They were startled to hear a painful groaning coming from inside and once again vacated the area. This time they did not return, deciding to leave the Spring Valley Vampire to someone else.

Since that time, reports of the vampire have been eerily active. In spite of this, most people believe the weird creature is nothing more than the stuff of urban legend and the product of overactive teenage imagination. That's what many people believe—but not everyone. Those who have reported encountering the creature firsthand are convinced that there is more to this story than meets the eye. These same people encourage an interest in the vampire—but warn against entering this cemetery after dark.

NORTHERN
ILLINOIS

I t is not an exaggeration to say that Northern Illinois owes its founding and prosperity to its rivers. It was not mere chance that the first white men to explore the upper Mississippi Valley passed through this region first. In days gone by, the waterways were of utmost importance for travel and exploration, and the rivers that connected upper Illinois with the Great Lakes were called one of the five great "keys to the continent."

The rivers became a method of moving military men and explorers, as well as a way of preventing—or in some cases enabling—Indian massacres. This region became a place with a brutal history, one where death and bloodshed left lingering impressions behind.

GHOSTS OF THE BARTONVILLE ASYLUM

If spirits are truly the personalities of those who once lived, then wouldn't these spirits reflect whatever turmoil might have plagued them in life? And if hauntings might sometimes be the effects of trauma being imprinted on the atmosphere of a place, then wouldn't places where terror and insanity were commonplace be especially prone to these hauntings? To find answers to both of these questions, you need look no further than to the strange events that have plagued the old Peoria State Hospital in Bartonville, a small town near Peoria, for many years.

In its final years of operations, after the last patients had departed, staff members who remained started to report some odd occurrences. In more recent years, the building has been the site of frequent excursion by vandals, trespassers, and curiosity seekers, many of whom claim to have had their own weird encounters in the place.

But what macabre history is behind this now-crumbling building? There are many tales to tell about this sad and forlorn place, strange stories filled with insanity, social reform, and apparently even ghosts.

Prior to 1900, mental health care barely existed. In those days, anyone suffering from a mental disorder was simply locked away from society in an asylum. Many of these hospitals were filthy places of confinement where patients were often left in straitjackets, locked in restraint chairs, or even placed in crates or cages if they were especially disturbed. Many of them spent every day in shackles and chains, and even the so-called treatments were barbaric.

Not surprisingly, such techniques brought little success, and patients rarely improved. In these days before psychiatry and medication, most mental patients spent their entire lives locked up inside an asylum. Things began to change around 1905, when new laws were passed and psychiatry began to promote the fact that the mentally ill could actually be helped, not just locked away and forgotten.

One man who was a leader in this social reform was Dr. George A. Zeller, who became the first superintendent of the Bartonville asylum in 1898. He served in the Spanish-American War, worked as the Illinois State Alienist, and then served at Bartonville until his death in 1938. He is remembered today as one of the most influential mental health care providers in Illinois history.

Construction was completed at the Bartonville asylum in 1902 and opened under the leadership of Dr. Zeller. It was called the Peoria State Hospital, named for the closest large town. The hospital implemented what was called the cottage system, with thirty-three different buildings used to house patients, as well as a dorm for the nursing staff, store, powerhouse, and domestic building with laundry, bakery, and kitchen. Dr. Zeller also supervised the creation of cemeteries, where the bodies of unknown patients could be buried. Eventually the burial grounds grew to include four different graveyards, although it was the oldest cemetery that marked the location of the first ghost story ever to be associated with the hospital. And this is no mere rumor or folktale, but a documented account of a supernatural event by Dr. George A. Zeller himself.

Shortly after organizing the cemeteries for the hospital, Dr. Zeller put together a burial corps to deal with the disposal of the bodies of patients who died. The corps consisted of a staff member and several of the patients. Though the patients were disturbed, all of them were competent enough to take part in the digging of graves. Of all the gravediggers, the most unusual man, according to Dr. Zeller, was a fellow called "A. Bookbinder."

This man had been sent to the hospital from a county poorhouse. He had suffered a mental breakdown while working in a printing house in Chicago, and his illness had left him incapable of coherent speech. The officer who had taken him into custody noted in his report that the man had been employed as "a bookbinder." A court clerk inadvertently listed this as the man's name, and he was sent to the hospital as A. Bookbinder.

Dr. Zeller described the man as being strong and healthy, although completely uncommunicative. He was attached to the burial corps, and soon attendants realized that Bookbinder was especially suited to the work. Ordinarily, as the coffin was lowered at the end of the funeral, the gravedigger would stand back out of the way until the service ended. Nearly every patient at the hospital was unknown to the staff, so services were performed out of respect for the deceased and not because of some personal attachment. Because of this, everyone was surprised during the first interment attended by Bookbinder when he removed his cap and began to weep loudly for the dead man.

"The first few times he did this," Dr. Zeller wrote, "his emotion became contagious and there were many moist eyes at the graveside but when at each succeeding burial, his feelings overcame him, it was realized that Old Book possessed a mania that manifested itself in uncontrollable grief."

It was soon learned that Bookbinder had no favorites among the dead. He would do the same thing at each service, and as his grief reached its peak, he would go and lean against an old elm tree that stood in the center of the cemetery, where he would sob loudly.

Time passed and eventually Bookbinder also passed away. Word spread among the employees, and as Book was well liked, they all decided they would attend his funeral. Dr. Zeller wrote that more than a hundred uniformed nurses attended, along with male staff members and several hundred patients.

Dr. Zeller officiated at the service. Bookbinder's casket was placed on two crossbeams above his empty grave, and four men stood by to lower it into the ground at the end of the service. As the last hymn was sung, the men grabbed hold of the ropes. "The men stooped forward," Dr. Zeller wrote, "and with a powerful, muscular effort, prepared to lift the coffin, in order to permit the removal of the crossbeams and allow it to gently descend into the grave. At a given signal, they heaved away the ropes and the next instant, all four lay on their backs. For the coffin, instead of offering resistance, bounded into the air like an eggshell, as if it were empty!"

Needless to say, the spectators were a little shocked at this turn of events, and the nurses were reported to have shrieked, half of them running away and the other half coming closer to the grave to see what was happening.

"In the midst of the commotion," Dr. Zeller continued, "a wailing voice was heard and every eye turned toward the Graveyard Elm from whence it emanated. Every man and woman stood transfixed, for there, just as had always been the case, stood Old Book, weeping and moaning with an earnestness that outrivaled anything he had ever shown before." Dr. Zeller was amazed at what he observed but had no doubt that he was actually seeing it. "I, along with the other bystanders, stood transfixed at the sight of this apparition . . . it was broad daylight and there could be no deception."

After a few moments, the doctor summoned some men to remove the lid of the coffin, convinced that it must be empty and that Old Book could not be inside it. The lid was lifted, and as soon as it was, the wailing sound came to an end. Inside the casket lay the body of Old Book, unquestionably dead. It was said that every eye in the cemetery looked upon the still corpse and then over to the elm tree in the center of the burial ground. The specter had vanished!

"It was awful, but it was real," Dr. Zeller concluded. "I saw it, 100 nurses saw it, and 300 spectators saw it." If it were anything other than the ghost of Old Book, Dr. Zeller had no idea what it could have been.

A few days after the funeral, the Graveyard Elm began to wither and die. In spite of efforts to save it, the tree declined over the next year and then died. Later, after the dead limbs had dropped, workmen tried to remove the rest of the tree, but they stopped after the first cut of the ax caused the tree to emanate what was said to be "an agonized, despairing cry of pain." After that, Dr. Zeller suggested that the tree be burned. As soon as the flames started around the tree base, however, the workers quickly put them out. They later told Dr. Zeller they had heard a sobbing and crying sound coming from the tree.

Eventually the tree fell down in a storm, taking with it the lingering memories of a mournful man known as A. Bookbinder.

After the death of Dr. Zeller, the hospital remained in use for many years, adding buildings, patients, and care facilities for children and tuberculosis patients. It was finally closed down in 1972 and remained empty for a number of years before being sold at auction in 1980.

Even though the site is now private property, it has not stopped vandals and would-be ghost hunters from going inside the place. Many of these curiosity seekers, drawn to the building because of its legends and ghosts, claim to have encountered some pretty frightening things here, from unexplained sounds to full-blown apparitions. Some might even say that many of the former patients are still around.

So is the old hospital really haunted? Scores of people who have visited the place certainly think so. As a building where mentally ill people were housed and "psychic disturbances" would have been common, the place certainly has the potential for a haunting, even without the story of A. Bookbinder and the Graveyard Elm. The atmosphere alone is more than enough to justify the reports of apparitions and strange energy. Also, hospitals have long been places where the spirits of the dead are said to linger. Besides that, some would say that the asylum was the only home that many of the patients knew, and it seems that some spirits are drawn to stay where they were the most comfortable.

"The place is full of spirits" has been said of the Bartonville asylum on more than one occasion, and it would not be surprising if this proclamation were right.

THE HOUSE WITH NO SQUARE CORNERS

Near the tiny town of Bull Valley is perhaps one of the strangest houses in Northern Illinois. Originally located far off the beaten path, it remains secluded today along a quiet and mostly deserted country highway. When George and Sylvia Stickney built this English country house in the mid-1800s, they chose this isolated place for the peace and quiet as well as for their spiritualistic activities. Both of them were said to be accomplished mediums, and they wanted to host parties and séances for their friends.

The house itself was very unusual in its design. It was two stories high, although the second floor was reserved for a ballroom that ran the entire length of the building. During the Civil War, the house also served as quarters for Federal soldiers, and it was home to the first piano in McHenry County. But this was not why the house gained its fame—or rather, its notoriety.

As devout practitioners of Spiritualism, the Stickneys insisted on adding distinctive features in the design of the house. These features, they assured the architect, would assist them when holding séances and gatherings at the property. They specified that the house should have no square corners, explaining that spirits have a tendency to get stuck in these corners, which could have dire results.

According to legend, though, one corner of a room accidentally ended up with a 90-degree measurement. How this could have happened is unknown. Perhaps the architect either forgot or was unable to complete the room with anything but right angle. This single square corner gave rise to an eerie legend of the house.

As the story goes, it was in this corner that George Stickney was discovered one day. He was slumped to the floor, dead of apparent heart failure, although no visible signs suggested a cause of death. Was he right about the square corners? Could an angry ghost, summoned by a séance, have been trapped in the corner?

After the death of her husband, Sylvia lived on in the house and gained considerable fame as a spirit medium. The upstairs ballroom was converted into a large séance chamber, and people came from far and wide to contact the spirits.

Time passed, and despite the séances and the mysterious death of George Stickney, no one considered the house to be haunted until the late 1970s. Then a real estate listing for the house was printed that seemed to show a woman in a white gown pulling aside a curtain and peering out. The photographer who took the picture said that no one was in the house at the time.

Eventually the house was sold, and the next owners claimed to experience nothing unusual in the place. They stayed on for several years but moved out when their plans to restore the mansion didn't pan out. Their occupancy left nothing to suggest that they were bothered by ghosts, and apparently neither are the owners today. The local Police Department uses a portion of the restored house as its headquarters and claims nothing out of the ordinary. The official word is that although the house was badly treated by vandals, it is not now nor was it ever haunted.

So who knows? Some area residents dispute the final word from the authorities. They say that ghostly things have been going on in the Stickney Mansion for many years, and continue to go on today, whether or not the local police officers want to admit it. What is the truth? No one seems to be able to say, and the ghosts, if there are any here, are certainly not talking.

ECHOES FROM THE PAST AT VISHNU SPRINGS

Hidden away in a secluded valley along the Lamoine River in McDonough County is a secret place, one long forgotten by the outside world. It was once considered a magical valley by those who came here seeking peace, serenity, and the healing waters of the springs. Today Vishnu Springs is an abandoned village of which no homes, streets, or residents remain. Only a once stately three-story hotel stands as testimony to days gone by. But though Illinois history has forgotten Vishnu Springs, it seems that Vishnu Springs has not forgotten the events that once took place here. They linger behind as ghostly echoes from the past.

The shady valley had always attracted the early pioneers of the region, who used the quiet spot as a place to picnic. It was not long before many residents of the nearby town of Colchester began to realize that the water in the valley was different from the drinking water that could be found elsewhere. The spring water was said to have a peculiar salt content, seven medicinal properties, and an especially appealing taste. People began coming from near and far to sample the water, hauling away jugs of it from the springs. Allegedly doctors sent their patients here on crutches, and they walked away without them.

By the 1880s, the owner of the property, Darius Hicks, began to realize its potential. He named the place Vishnu after reading about the 1861 discovery of Angkor, an abandoned city perfectly preserved for 300 years by vegetation growing out of the Krishna River. Vishnu was a Hindu god whose earthly incarnation was said to be the river that had covered Angkor.

Eventually Hicks decided that this would make a perfect place to start a town. He was the first to see the opportunity to create a town here, but sadly, it never met his expectations. Hicks's own problems drove him to self-destruction, and by the 1920s, the once thriving place was virtually abandoned.

Hicks came from a local wealthy family, and he and his brother managed the family land. It was on one of these sections of land that he became acquainted with the rich mineral springs that later became Vishnu. He was toiling in the fields one hot summer day and wandered into the shady valley for a drink of water. Almost immediately, he fell under the spell of the place. He later began marketing and selling the water.

In 1889, he became quite aware of what the springs had to offer, but he also realized that he would reap their benefits at a price. As nearly 3,000 people came to attend a camp meeting at Vishnu, the devoted trampled down an entire field of Hicks's corn and frightened a prize bull so badly that it disappeared. Hicks now had to choose whether to farm the land or develop it. Instead of farming, he chose to build a town. The first new building was the Capitol Hotel, which offered rooms for those who came to the health resort. Hicks publicized the springs, and soon land was purchased and other projects followed.

By the following spring, Vishnu had three stores, a restaurant, livery stable and blacksmith, and photo gallery. Hicks organized the Vishnu Transfer Line, which made trips from Colchester to the new resort. For the cost of 75 cents, a passenger could be transported to Vishnu, have dinner, and then be transported back.

Although local newspapers reported that Vishnu was an idyllic boomtown, there was an undercurrent of trouble at the springs. Hicks evidently did not get along well with his developer, Charles K. Way, and there was talk of dividing the community into two parts. Way eventually developed land southeast of the hotel. Also, the resort became known for the sale and consumption of illegal alcohol (Colchester and the county were both dry at that time), and the drinking on the grounds of the resort led to occasional fights.

Meanwhile, despite the drinking and violence, Hicks continued to develop the resort as a place of peace and healing. He had a new organ installed in the hotel parlor, and the building boasted a number of other improvements, including running water and an elevator to reach the third-floor ballroom. Amusements were added for the resort travelers, such as a real horse-powered carousel, and the lawn around the hotel was fitted with swings, hammocks, a croquet grounds, a picnic area, and a large pond that was dubbed Lake Vishnu and stocked with goldfish. Hicks also built a racetrack and established a park, both of which were not in the valley but on a nearby hill. Additionally, he promoted and arranged for cultural activities like dances, band concerts, and holiday celebrations.

While Hicks struggled to create a viable community at the springs, his personal life was filled with problems. In 1889, Hicks had gotten married for a second time, to Hattie Rush of Missouri, one of the many pilgrims who had traveled to Vishnu in search of healing waters She had also been married before and had children of her own, including a twelve-year-old daughter named Maud. Hattie suffered from Bright's disease and was plagued with heart trouble. She died in 1896 at the age of only forty.

Whether his marriage to Hattie had been happy or not, Hicks then went on to do something that scandalized those in the region for some years to come—he married his stepdaughter. Maud became the third Mrs. Hicks in September 1897 in a private civil ceremony at the McDonough County courthouse. She was only twenty years old at the time. Although the marriage was not actually incestuous, it was seen as improper, and Hicks was shunned by the more conservative members of the community. In 1898, Maud gave birth to a son, and in 1903, she had a daughter. In just two years, though, Maud would be dead, and a curse seemed to settle over the struggling, yet peaceful community of Vishnu Springs.

In 1903, two events occurred that led to the final decline of Vishnu. One warm summer day, the owner of the children's carousel was crushed to death when his shirt sleeve somehow became caught in the gears. When the ride stopped that day, it never ran again.

Later that same year, Maud Hicks gave birth to another daughter, but both she and the child died during the delivery. Maud's death was a tremendous shock to Darius Hicks. He certainly never dreamed that his wife, who was twenty-seven years younger than he, would precede him to the grave. On the day following Maud's funeral, he took his young son and daughter and turned his back on Vishnu—never to return. But his troubles were not over yet . . .

After leaving Vishnu, Hicks bought a farm a short distance away and took up residence there. He hired as a housekeeper a widow named Nellie Darrah, who was needed to help care for his two young children. In the years that followed, Nellie became a mother figure to the children and became romantically involved with Hicks. By the winter of 1908, Nellie had become pregnant and confronted Hicks, demanding that he marry her. He refused and she subsequently had an abortion. The procedure did not go well, and she had to be hospitalized.

While in the hospital, Nellie contacted Hicks and threatened to publicize their entire affair. Hicks never replied to her threats, but he took a .32-caliber rifle and shot himself in the head, dying at the age of only fifty-eight.

The death of Darius Hicks also sounded a death knell for Vishnu Springs. He had been the main promoter of the town and had remained involved in the business of his hotel, even after moving away. Hicks's death sent the community into a decline from which it never recovered.

The hotel and the town, now under indifferent management, began to attract gamblers, thieves, and criminals. On one occasion, a huge number of counterfeit half-dollars, which looked like the real thing but were made from pewter, were seized there. There were other stories of lawbreakers captured at Vishnu, and legend has it that some of their loot remains hidden in the caves that surround the valley.

Eventually the property was sold and left to decay. By the 1920s, Vishnu was nothing more than a legend-haunted ghost town, abandoned and forgotten in the secluded valley. Vandals stole valuable hotel furnishings and broke the windows of the buildings. By the 1930s, the hotel had decayed into little more than a shell, and the owner, a local banker, lost all of his property during the

Depression. It seemed that the curse that plagued Vishnu was continuing to wreak havoc.

In 1935, a restoration effort was started by Ira Post, who bought the hotel and 220 acres around it. He restored the building and hired a caretaker. They opened the former resort as a picnic grounds, and though it met with a limited amount of success, Vishnu would never be a community again. Post and his family lived at the hotel for weeks at a time, overseeing the work that was being done. He died in 1951, and though the hotel was occasionally rented in the years after, the grounds became overgrown and unkempt. Soon it was completely abandoned once more.

In the early 1970s, Vishnu Springs saw life again as a sort of commune for a group of Western Illinois University graduates and their friends. They turned the hotel into their home and sacrificed their professional careers to live with nature. Earning enough money to pay the rent and the expensive winter heating bills, the group gardened and raised livestock to make ends meet, occasionally hosting music festivals and parties. But eventually they too were gone, and Vishnu was once again deserted.

As the years have passed, the old hotel has continued to deteriorate, and today it is little more than a crumbling shadow of its former self. Despite the interest of local societies and historic groups, the valley remained private property until the death of the last member of the Post family. Since that time, the status of the land has remained in limbo, and the ultimate fate of Vishnu remains a mystery.

And perhaps it is this very mystery, as well as its isolation, that has been the source of the stories that have been told about Vishnu. As the town fell into ruin and the houses collapsed and were covered with weeds and brush, those who ventured into Vishnu came away with strange and perplexing tales. Some reported seeing a woman in black roaming through the abandoned streets. Who this woman may have been is unknown, but she was said to vanish without a trace when approached. Visitors also told of sounds from Vishnu's past echoing into the present—the sounds of voices, laughter, and music, as if the glory days of Vishnu were still being lived out in a world just beyond our own.

And apparently the sounds of everyday life continue here as well. One person who visited the hotel heard the sound of someone pounding on metal coming from outside. After I showed him an old map of Vishnu, he realized the sounds were coming from the direction of the old livery barn and blacksmith shop. No trace of this building remains today, and no hammers and anvils can be found among the ruins of Vishnu.

Is Vishnu Springs a haunted place? Perhaps not in the traditional sense, as aside from the legendary woman in black, there are no ghostly apparitions to be found wandering in the darkness. Nevertheless, how can we explain the eerie sounds that have been reported by several generations of visitors to this quiet place?

If you go there, be careful how you step in Vishnu, and leave nothing of what you bring behind. Years ago, Ira Post's niece and daughter erected a sign at the entrance to Vishnu, and though the sign is gone now, the sentiment behind it remains. It read in part: "Vishnu Springs was preserved as planned by Ira Post. The spring water of the wonderful world of nature is left to enjoy . . . the springs should be left as nature provided it. Take care of it all and then all will be benefited in the years to come. Ira Post died in 1951. The wishes expressed here were his. Help us to see that his wishes are carried out."

PHANTOM MONKS

Archer Avenue, which runs through Northern Illinois on a southwestern route between Chicago and Lemont, is undoubtedly one of the most haunted stretches of road in the state. There are a number of locations along this road, including cemeteries, homes, and businesses, that boast more than their share of ghosts. This old Indian trail was turned into an actual road in the 1830s. Irish workers on the Illinois-Michigan Canal completed the construction.

Along Archer Avenue is the St. James-Sag Church and burial ground, which date back a number of years before the road was built to follow the route of the canal. Most of the men who worked on the road and canal moved out of Chicago and became parishioners of the church. The site of the church and burial grounds has a long history in the Chicago area. The site marks the second-oldest Catholic church in Northern Illinois and dates back to 1833. Before that, French explorers Marquette and Jolliet were the first white men to see this area, later known as the Sag Ridge. When they arrived in 1673, the local Indians were using it as a burial ground. The site became a mission and a French signal post in the late 1600s. The present parish was established not by the French, but by the Irish when so many of them moved into the region as workers on the canal.

The first church was constructed in 1833, a simple log cabin that stood on the highest point of the ridge. In 1850, it was replaced by the limestone building that is still in use today. On top of the hill, just a short distance from the newer rectory, the pale yellow building stands watch over the hundreds of graves scattered about on the hills below.

Supernatural events have been reported at St. James-Sag since around 1847. It was at this time when the first sightings of the phantom monks took place there. These stories continued for decades, and there were many reliable witnesses to the strange activity. One of them, a former rector of the church, admitted on his deathbed that he had seen ghosts roaming the cemetery grounds for many years.

One cold night in November 1977, a Cook County police officer was passing the cemetery and happened to turn his spotlight past the cemetery gates. He claimed that he saw nine hooded figures floating up the cemetery road toward the rectory. Knowing that no one was supposed to be in the cemetery, he stopped and yelled out the window at them to come back toward the road. If they did not, they would be arrested for trespassing. The figures simply ignored him and continued up the road toward the church and rectory.

Quickly, he grabbed his shotgun and ran around the gate and into the graveyard. He pursued what he first thought were pranksters into the cemetery, but while he stumbled and fell over the uneven ground and tombstones, the monklike figures eerily glided past without effort. He said that he had nearly caught up with them when they simply vanished. Unable to believe what had just happened, he searched around the area for any trace of the figures, but found no one. Finally he returned to his squad car to write up his report. The paperwork that he filed merely stated that he had chased some trespassers through the cemetery, but he always maintained that what he had seen was from beyond this world.

THE WATSEKA WONDER

The small town of Watseka is located about fifty miles south of Chicago and on the eastern side of the state, just a few miles from the Indiana border. The sensation that came to be known as the Watseka Wonder first made its appearance here in July 1877.

At this time a thirteen-year-old girl named Lurancy Vennum fell into a strange, catatonic sleep, during which she claimed to speak with spirits. The attacks occurred many times each day and sometimes lasted as long as eight hours. During her trance, Lurancy would speak in different voices, although when she awoke, she would remember nothing. News of the strange girl traveled about the state, and many visitors came to see her.

Finally doctors diagnosed Lurancy as being mentally ill, and they recommended that she be sent to the state insane asylum in Peoria. In January 1878, a man named Asa Roff, also from Watseka, came to visit the Vennum family. He claimed that his own daughter, Mary, had been afflicted with the same condition as Lurancy. He was convinced that his daughter had actually spoken to spirits. In addition, he was also convinced that his daughter's spirit still existed, and he soon discovered that she apparently was communicating through Lurancy.

Mary Roff had died on the afternoon of July 5, 1865, while hospitalized at the Peoria asylum. She had been committed after a bizarre incident when she began slashing at her arms with a straight razor. It was the final tragedy in Mary's descent into madness and insanity. In the beginning, it had only been strange voices that filled her head. Next, she experienced long periods when she stayed in a trancelike state. Then came her moments of awakening, when she spoke in other voices and seemed to be possessed by the spirits of other people. Finally she developed an obsession with blood. Mary was convinced that she needed to remove the blood from her body, using pins, leeches, and at last, a sharpened razor. After that final incident, her parents took her to the asylum. Mary endured the treatments for insanity that existed at the time and died a short time later.

At the time of Mary Roff's death, Lurancy Vennum was a little more than one year old. In just over a decade, though, their lives became forever connected in a case that remains today one of the strangest, and most authentic, cases of possession ever recorded.

Lurancy Vennum was born on April 16, 1864, and she and her family moved to Watseka when she was seven years old. Since they arrived long after Mary Roff's death, the Vennum family knew nothing of the girl or her family. Then on July 11, 1877, a series of strange events began.

On that morning, Lurancy complained to her mother about feeling sick, and then collapsed onto the floor. She stayed in a deep, catatonic sleep for the next five hours, but when she awoke, she seemed fine. The next day, Lurancy once again slipped off into the trancelike sleep, but this time was different, as she began speaking aloud of visions and spirits. In her trance, she told her family that she was in heaven and could see and hear spirits, including the spirit of her brother, who had died in 1874.

From that day on, the trances began to occur more frequently and would sometimes last for hours. While she was asleep, Lurancy continued to speak about her visions, which were sometimes terrifying. She claimed that spirits were chasing her through the house and shouting her name. The attacks occurred up to a dozen times each day, and as they continued, Lurancy began to speak in other languages, or at least in nonsense words that no one could understand. When she awoke, she would remember nothing of her trance or strange ramblings.

The stories and rumors about Lurancy and her visions began to circulate in Watseka. No one followed the case more closely than Asa Roff. In the early stages of Mary's illness, she too had claimed to communicate with spirits and would fall into long trances without warning. He was sure that Lurancy Vennum was suffering from the same illness as his daughter. But Roff said nothing until the Vennum family had exhausted every known cure for Lurancy. It was not until the local doctor and a minister suggested that the girl be sent to the state mental hospital that Roff got involved.

On January 31, 1878, he contacted the Vennum family. They were naturally skeptical of his story, but he persuaded them to let him bring Dr. E. Winchester Stevens to the house. Stevens, like Roff, was a dedicated Spiritualist, and the two men had become convinced that Lurancy was not insane. They believed that Lurancy was actually a vessel through which the dead were communicating. Roff only wished that he had seen the same evidence in his own daughter years before.

The Vennums allowed Dr. Stevens to "mesmerize" the girl and try to contact the spirits through her. Within moments, Lurancy was speaking in another voice, which allegedly came from a spirit named Katrina Hogan. Then the spirit changed and claimed to be that of Willie Canning, a young man who had committed suicide. She spoke as Willie for more than an hour, and then suddenly she threw her arms into the air and fell over backward. Dr. Stevens took her hands, and soon Lurancy calmed and gained control of her body again. She was now in heaven and would allow a gentler spirit to control her.

She said the spirit's name was Mary Roff.

The trance continued on into the next day, and by this time, Lurancy apparently had become Mary Roff. She said that she wanted to leave the Vennum house, which was unfamiliar to her, and go home to the Roff house. When Mrs. Roff heard the news, she hurried to the Vennum house in the company of her married daughter, Minerva Alter. The two women came up the sidewalk and saw Lurancy sitting by the window. "Here comes Ma and Nervie," she reportedly said, and ran up to hug the two surprised women. No one had called Minerva by the name "Nervie" since Mary's death in 1865.

It now seemed evident to everyone involved that Mary had taken control of Lurancy. Although she looked the same, she knew everything about the Roff family and treated them as her loved ones. The Vennums, on the other hand, although treated very courteously, were viewed with a distant politeness.

On February 11, Lurancy, or rather "Mary," was allowed to go home with the Roffs. Mr. and Mrs. Vennum agreed that it would be for the best, although they desperately hoped that Lurancy would regain her true identity.

The Roffs took Lurancy across town, and as they traveled, they passed by the former Roff home, where they had been living when Mary died. She demanded to know why they were not returning there, and they had to explain that they had moved a few years back.

For the next several months, Lurancy lived as Mary and seemed to have completely forgotten her former life. She did, however, tell her mother that she would be with them only until "some time in May." As days passed, Lurancy continued to show that she knew more about the Roff family, their possessions, and habits than she could possibly have known if she had been faking the whole thing. Many of the incidents and remembrances that she referred to had taken place years before Lurancy had even been born.

In early May, Lurancy told the Roff family that it was time for her to leave. She became very sad and despondent and would spend the day going from one family member to the next, hugging them and touching them at every opportunity.

Finally, on May 21, Lurancy returned home to the Vennums. She displayed none of the strange symptoms of her earlier illness, and her parents were convinced that somehow she had been cured, thanks to intervention by the spirit of Mary Roff. She soon became a happy and healthy young woman, suffering no ill effects from her strange experience.

She remained in touch with the Roff family for the rest of her life. Although she had no memories of her time as Mary, she still felt a curious closeness to them that she could never really explain.

Eight years later, when Lurancy turned eighteen, she married a local farmer named George Binning, and two years later, they moved to Rawlins County, Kansas. They bought a farm there and had eleven children. Lurancy died in the late 1940s while she was in California visiting one of her daughters.

Asa Roff and his wife received hundreds of letters, from believers and skeptics alike, after the story of the possession was printed on the front page of the Watseka newspaper. After a year of constant hounding and scorn from neighbors, they left Watseka and moved to Emporia, Kansas. Seven years later, they returned to Watseka to live with Minerva and her husband. They died of old age and are buried in Watseka.

Mary Roff was never heard from again.

So what really happened in Watseka? Did Mary Roff's spirit really possess the body of Lurancy Vennum? The families of everyone involved certainly thought so. From all accounts, Lurancy had the memories and personality of a girl who had been dead for more than twelve years. What other explanation could possibly exist for what happened?

THE MAPLE LAKE GHOST LIGHT

Maple Lake is a tranquil reservoir at the swampy north end of the Sag Ridge. Just outside Willow Springs is part of a line of forest preserves that follows the Des Plaines River. By day, it is a widely used recreational area, but at night, long after the sun has gone down, it becomes home to one of the most famous "spook lights" in the Chicagoland region.

The land where Maple Lake now lies was once owned by an Irish immigrant named James Molony. He was one of the early parishioners of the St. James-Sag Church and owned about eighty acres around 95th Street and Wolf Road. Members of the family owned this property from 1850 until it was taken over by the Forest Preserve District around 1920. At that time, the area from Archer Avenue southward was known as Maple Hill, thanks to the large number of sugar maple trees that were found on the land.

In 1924, the Forest Preserve contracted for the construction of a dam across a deep, narrow ravine that provided an outlet for a number of acres of swampland south of 95th Street and east of Wolf Road. The area that was submerged because of the dam came to be called Maple Lake.

Swimming became a popular pastime along the south shore at the west end of Maple Lake until about 1939, when it was finally banned. In recent times, the lake has continued to have appeal to picnickers, hikers, boaters, and fishermen. The setting here is quiet and picturesque, and it offers much to outdoor enthusiasts during the daylight hours. At night, though, things look much different at Maple Lake. The towering trees that are so awe-inspiring during the daytime become foreboding and ominous in the darkness. The vast expanse of the lake, so clear and crystal blue in the sunlight, becomes a vast expanse of blackness after the sun sets.

Many nighttime visitors are attracted to the lake because of the accounts of the ghost light that is said to appear here. This light can be seen out over the water between 95th and 107th Streets, most often along the northern edge of the lake, across from the Maple Lake Overlook. It is from here that visitors have reported witnessing a red light that moves slowly along the edge of the water on the far side of the lake. The light is always round and burns a brilliant red. It is often so bright that it casts a glare down onto the water before it.

No one knows for sure what this anomaly may be, but legends abound. The most familiar of the stories surrounding the Maple Lake spook light claims that a Native American was beheaded near the lake and now is seen as the ghost light, searching for his missing head. A variation purports that the headless ghost is that of an early settler who was attacked and killed by Indians, and the strange light is his lantern as he wanders the shoreline in a search of his head. But no theory can point to a documented event that has taken place near Maple Lake that can explain the eerie light—until now.

The land where Maple Lake is now located was once owned by James Molony, who built a house on the property that is now Forest Preserve land surrounding Maple Lake. His home stood until about 1970 and was used by the Forest Preserve District until it burned down. Its foundation is still visible today, just off the Bull Frog Lake parking lot west of Maple Lake. This was not the first site where Molony planned to build his home, however. That location is now covered by the lake, and Molony abandoned the site after a tragic event occurred there in 1858.

Molony had come from Ireland in the 1850s and had been given the management of a small store that supplied the woodcutters who were clearing the path for the canal. He met, fell in love with, and became engaged to a young woman named Ellen Connelly, and Molony began seeking out a site on which to build a home for himself and his bride. He soon found a pleasant location and purchased it with his savings. He chose a spot where the house would be built, and as the first improvement of the land, Molony began digging a well.

He and the workmen that he hired had gone down about eighty feet but laid off work on the morning of October 8, 1858, to attend the christening of a baby boy named Michael Scanlon who had been born in the neighborhood. Festivities and drinking followed the gathering, and during the party, Molony invited several of his friends to go over and inspect his new well.

One of the men climbed into the bucket that was being used by the workers and asked to be let down into the well. Before he had reached the bottom, he fell out of the bucket, to the delight of his friends. The men had all had too much to drink, but one of the friends climbed into the bucket and went down in search of the first man. He also fell out of the bucket.

James Molony decided to go down and look for the two men, but one of his friends warned him that they might have been affected by the "damps," which occurred in mines that were dug in swampy areas. With no word from the men below, another man volunteered to go down, stating that he would call for help if he found any gas. He never had the chance. He was overwhelmed by gas and died, still in the bucket.

Resigned to the fact that the men below were lost, the others tracked down a heavy rope and a grappling hook and managed to snag and retrieve the bodies of the dead men, one at a time. The women gathered as the men worked late into the night, illuminating the area with candles and oil lamps. At last, by the dim glow of the lights, the corpses were laid out on the ground, and a priest came to serve the final rites. The men were buried a few days later at the cemetery on Sag Ridge.

After the horrific loss of his friends, Molony had the well filled in, and he built his house on one of the hills across the basin. He wanted nothing more to do with this cursed piece of ground.

If a paranormal explanation need be found as to the cause of the Maple Lake ghost light, this morbid incident certainly was a real and terrible event that occurred where the light is now seen. But is the light natural or supernatural? None can say with authority, but one thing is certain—if history does create modern-day hauntings, then Maple Lake certainly has the history to go along with its ghost.

ELVIRA OF THE WOODSTOCK OPERA HOUSE

Woodstock is a quaint little town in Northern Illinois. The town surrounds a historic community square that is lined with preserved, turn-of-the-century homes and buildings, not the least of which is the towering Woodstock Opera House. It looms more than four stories above the rest of the downtown, its highest point being the bell tower, which is more than two and a half stories in itself.

Over the years, the Opera House has played host to many well-known actors and actresses. When it first opened in 1890, the first performers were the Patti Rose Players, who billed themselves as the leading opera company in the Midwest. Since that time, many renowned stars have appeared here, including Orson Welles, Shelley Berman, Tom Bosley, Betsy Palmer, Lois Nettleton, Geraldine Page, and Paul Newman.

The one thing that the Opera House has that most other theaters do not is an in-house critic. In Woodstock, she always makes her opinions known during dress rehearsals. If a play does not meet her standards, she will rush into the balcony like a temperamental director and begin slamming seats up and down. Who is this obnoxious critic? Her name, according to theater legends, is Elvira, and she is none other than the theater's oldest patron. She had been around the place as long as anyone can remember, dating back to at least the 1890s. She is not an elderly ticket buyer—she is the Opera House's resident ghost!

Who Elvira may be is unknown. Some believe she was an actress who committed suicide by jumping from the theater's tower, either because of a doomed love affair or because she did not get the choice role that she wanted. Regardless, she haunts the theater today. Tradition has it that the ghost holds claim to the seat DD 113. It is said to be her favorite, and the theater manager admits that it is the most requested seat in the house. Even when the rest of the balcony is empty, including the better seats, someone always wants to sit in Elvira's seat.

Although most consider Elvira to be a friendly spirit, she can make herself known in some pretty unnerving ways. Scenery flats have suddenly toppled over during rehearsals, even though they are securely tied. Props sometimes shift location or simply fall over with no explanation. Strangest of all are the odd sounds from the balcony. It has been said that when things are not going particularly well during a rehearsal, Elvira lets out a long sigh of distaste from her favorite seat.

Today the Opera House continues to be an outstanding showplace and a popular theater. Apparently the stories of a resident ghost have not hurt the attendance. If anything, they seem to draw people who have not attended the theater before. With that in mind, it is interesting to note that even though she has been dead for more than a century, Elvira is finally fulfilling her dreams of becoming famous!

THE LIBRARY CURSE AND "OLD LADY GRAY"

Every town has its ghost stories, strange happenings, and mysterious events. For more than a century now, whenever anyone discusses the supernatural in Peoria, talk always turns to the city's public library and the haunting curse that has long plagued the property. For many readers, ghosts and spirits seem within the realm of possibility, but their imagination is stretched to the limit when asked to believe in the validity of a curse. If you are such a reader, keep your skepticism in check for just a bit longer—you may soon become a believer.

Andrew and Mary Gray first came to Peoria in the 1830s. The Irish immigrants bought a parcel of land, built a two-story house at 105 North Monroe Street, and settled into the growing community. Andrew was a commissioner and forwarder, assisting newly arrived visitors in the shipment and placement of their household goods, and soon earned great respect for his hard work and industrious nature. Mary gained her own reputation. She was an avid gardener and lovingly cared for the ground around her home. Those who passed by often pointed and stared in awe at the patches of flowers, shrubs, and greenery that grew lushly around the house.

Late in the 1830s, Mary's brother died in a neighboring state and her teenage nephew came to live with the couple. He was a troubled and lazy young man. He refused to get a job and spent his days drinking and was often in trouble with the law. He was a source of constant grief and disappointment for Mary Gray.

Around the same time that Mary's nephew came to Peoria, a young attorney named David Davis also moved into the community. He opened a one-man law firm and his first client was Mary's problematic nephew. Davis quickly became a force to be reckoned with, building his reputation by repeatedly defeating the town attorney as he tried to prosecute the nephew for his exploits. Eventually, Davis became concerned about the debt that the Grays were incurring for his services and he decided to use the mortgage on the Gray's property to secure his attorney fees.

The mortgage was signed over to Davis and then the money came due, Davis asked for his attorney fees. The Grays refused to pay, and David filed a lawsuit against them. During the trial, the Grays angrily denied signing the papers, even though Mr. Gray's signature was plainly visible on the note. Davis introduced the notarized document at trial and easily won the suit.

Meanwhile, Mary had kicked her nephew out of their house, and he began wandering the streets of Peoria, cursing the family to anyone who would listen. He vanished and his body was later found floating in the Illinois River. The Grays were removed from their home and forced to find a new place to live. Local legend claims that, in her despair and anger, "Old Lady Gray" called on God to bear witness to the injustice that had been visited upon her family. She cursed the ground of her former home on Monroe Street with "thorns and thistles, ill luck, sickness and death to every owner and occupant."

David Davis was now the owner of the cursed property. The soil that had been so rich and fertile under the care of Mary Gray was now choked with weeds. The flowers died and the bushes and shrubs withered away. The house was abandoned and was soon overrun by rats. Locals not only feared the curse on the house, but stories also claimed that the ghost of Mary Gray's nephew haunted the place. Those who passed by at night claimed that they glimpsed him at the front door, crying and pleading for his aunt's forgiveness. No one would accept money to care for the house or to maintain the grounds and the once stately home became a ramshackle eyesore.

Mary's curse, it was said, extended beyond the house and yard. David Davis's law firm suffered after his triumph over the Grays. The couple had been well-liked in the community and most people pitied their misfortunes. Shortly after he obtained his judgment over the Grays, Davis moved to Bloomington and never returned.

The Gray house remained abandoned and one winter night, it inexplicably caught fire and burned to the ground. The townspeople gathered to try and put out the blaze, but they arrived too late. The stories claim that, as the house burned, some of them saw the figure of Mary Gray, writhing in the flames and laughing with delight over the house's destruction. Shortly after the fire, the land was sold to pay off the property taxes. It then sat empty for years, over-grown with choking weeds, and people often crossed the street instead of walking directly past it. It was as if they believed that the curse might affect them if they dared to walk too close to it.

Time passed and the legends faded. A new rooming house was later built on the site and one of the tenants was former Illinois Governor Thomas Ford and his wife, Frances. Ford had left office in 1846 and was in debt, aged beyond his years, and was now living in a house that had been built on cursed land. Those who watched one misfortune after another befall the family came to believe that the curse was wreaking havoc on them. The Fords' three daughters all died of consumption. Frances Ford died from cancer on October 12, 1850. Governor Ford followed his wife to the grave just three weeks later, a broken and forgotten man. In 1872, the Fords' son, Tom, was mistaken for a cattle rustler and he was killed. His brother, Swell, sought to avenge his brother's death, and killed several of the men responsible. He was also shot to death a short time later.

The house was abandoned again. No one dared to live in it. In time, it was demolished, and part of the land was purchased by a downstate grocer, who gave it to one of his father's former slaves, Tom Lindsay. After the Civil War, Lindsay built a small house on the exact same piece of land where the Gray home had once stood. Three months after it was completed, the house was struck by lightning and burned to the ground. After the fire, Lindsay was informed of the curse by some of his neighbors. Although he had a healthy respect for the supernatural, he needed a place to live so he built a new house on the land that he owned.

One of his friends, who had his own beliefs in the supernatural, gave Lindsay a gift for his new home—a mummified rabbit's foot, which was meant to bring good luck. He buried the rabbit's foot under the front door of the new house. And he didn't stop there. He also obtained horseshoes to be hung in every room of the house. Apparently, these precautions paid off for he was able to live on Monroe Street for the next twenty-five years, without incident.

After Tom Lindsay died, the land was purchased by a local businessman who built an ornate home on the site for his new wife. He did not fare as well as Lindsay had—his bride died within the year and tragic stories of the curse once again began to spread throughout Peoria.

The remaining part of the Gray property was purchased by a local banker, who built his own home on the land. He was soon married, and the happy couple was blessed by the arrival of a baby boy. Their happiness was short-lived. The young mother died soon after the baby was born and days later, her infant son followed her to the grave. The banker stayed on in the house.

Eventually, he recovered from his grief and remarried. His new wife also gave birth to a son, but this child also died. The young woman lost her sanity and spent the rest of her days in an asylum.

The next occupant of the old Gray property opened one of the mansions as a rooming house. His daughter drowned in Lake Peoria and his son was killed after a fall from a hot-air balloon. For a time, the house was occupied by a company that made women's hats, but they didn't stay there for long. They spent a great part of their time, they claimed, trying to locate the source of a strange and sickening odor that hung in the air. It became so foul, and drove away so many customers, that they finally moved out.

Then, in 1894, the land was sold again, and a new library building was erected on the site one year later.

But the curse of Old Lady Gray continued.

The library was built on land that once belonged to Anew and Mary Gray in 1895. Erastus S. Wilcox was appointed as the head librarian of the handsome three-story structure. He was a scholar and lecturer and a staid, conservative man who always wore formal attire in public, insisted that gentlemen remove their hats inside of the building, and frequently scolded vagrants or children who loitered in the halls or in the stairways.

Willcox was the next victim of the curse. While walking to the library on the afternoon of March 30, 1915, he was struck by a streetcar at the intersection of Main Street and Glen Oak Avenue. According to witness accounts, the streetcar had sounded its bell, but Willcox apparently did not hear it. The motorman managed to avoid hitting him directly, but the fender of the car knocked him down and he sprawled unconscious on the pavement. Willcox was taken to Proctor Hospital with a deep gash in the back of his head. He died a few hours later.

The curse had, many believed, claimed another victim—and Erastus Willcox would not be the last. Tragedy struck subsequent librarians. Willcox's successor, S. Patterson Prouse, attended a meeting of the library board on December 21, 1921. He showed no signs of illness during the afternoon meeting; however, just as the meeting was coming to an end, he was walking to the door and collapsed onto the floor. Dr. A. J. Foerter was summoned from his office across the street from the library and while he did everything that he could, he was unable to revive him. He later said that he believed Prouse was dead before his body hit the floor.

After the untimely death of Prouse, the board searched for a new librarian to take charge, reorganize the library, and deal with the growing number of volumes. They hired Dr. Edwin Wiley in May 1922, but he only lasted for two years. He committed suicide on October 20, 1924, after ingesting a large dose of arsenic.

It should come as no surprise that some locals attributed his madness and death to the Gray Curse. And there were other oddities that occurred at the library. In 1907, a school superintendent blew up a safe at the library to cover his embezzlement of school funds. At the time, the school district's offices were in the library. The library also became embroiled in a blackmail plot that followed the death of union organizer George McNear, Jr. His widow was told that the name of his killer would be revealed if she placed $1,000 in a special drawer on the library's third floor. Police arrested two men, father and son, William Anthony Gibson and William John Gibson, who retrieved the envelope. They had no clues as to the murder and claimed their appearance at the library was a coincidence. A jury didn't believe them and both men went to prison.

The current Peoria Public Library branch on Main Street opened in March 1968. The story of the curse is still part of the fabric of the library's history, despite the years that have passed and the many renovations that have taken place over the years. However, it seems that a curse is not all that haunts this branch of the library—the building is also said to be home to several ghosts.

Among the lingering spirits is the specter of Erastus Willcox, the doomed librarian who was struck by the streetcar. Visitors and staff members have reported seeing a man in early-1900s clothing walking down hallways or prowling about in the stacks.

There may be other ghosts, too. Staff members who have been in the basement claim that they have been startled by icy cold spots, or strange cool breezes that seem to come from nowhere. Books are heard falling off the shelves and crashing to the floor, even though no books have actually been disturbed. Doors open and close, lights turn on and off, and sometimes voices are heard in empty basement rooms. When the sounds are investigated, no one—among the living, at least—is found.

Who wanders the library? The victims of the legendary curse? Ill-fated librarians and property owners? Or perhaps a former staff member or two who after finding the library to be a wonderful place in life chose to return to their beloved books after death.

THE LINGERING SPIRIT OF SPRINGDALE CEMETERY

Peoria's historic Springdale Cemetery was established in 1851 and, tragically, has not always been considered a place of rest. The graveyard saw periods of decline, neglect, and vandalism, but has managed to endure as beautiful and fascinating city of the dead, made up of acres of tombstones, mausoleums, and rolling hills.

It is also a place of mystery.

There are many tales of ghosts and spirits that have emerged from the confines of Springdale Cemetery. Among them are the wandering Civil War phantoms that have been seen around Soldier's Hill, and the young girl in the nineteenth century dress that pops up from behind tombstones and playfully frightens visitors, only to disappear. Her childish laughter is sometimes heard echoing among the grave markers.

But there is no ghost of Springdale Cemetery that is as infamous as that of the "Lady in White," the tragic figure Mildred Hallmark, whose body was found in the cemetery after she was brutally murdered in 1935. Her ghost is now linked to one of the most sensational murders in the city's history and seems forever doomed to wander the grounds of Springdale Cemetery.

The site of Springdale Cemetery was chosen as a burial ground in 1851. When the cemetery opened, a streetcar trolley ran up Perry Street to the cemetery. By the 1870s, the streetcars were used to pull caskets and funeral parties out to the end of the tracks because the old dirt road to the cemetery often turned to mud, preventing carriages from getting through. When it started, Springdale was made up of 200 acres, which were surrounded by a wooden fence. Within two decades, there had been more than 7,000 burials in the cemetery.

Even from the earliest days, the cemetery went through periods of neglect. The graveyard became overgrown and choked with weeds, and vandals stole and knocked over gravestones. There were also accusations of mismanagement and embezzlement by past trustees. Eventually, a historic preservation foundation was organized by concerned citizens to save the cemetery and today, it is a place where the past truly comes alive and one can walk among the graves that hold the remains of city founders, leaders, and local dignitaries.

And it's also possible, if the tales are to be believed, that one can also come face-to-face with Springdale's resident spirit, the Lady in White.

Mildred Hallmark, age nineteen, a recent graduate of the Academy of Our Lady Catholic School in June 1935. The pretty, auburn-haired girl was born on April 19, 1916, the daughter of John and Esther Hallmark. The family had moved to Peoria in 1928. At the time of her murder, Mildred was working as a waitress at Bishop's Cafeteria in an area of town that boasted bars, theaters, and restaurants that ran the length of Main Street and beyond.

On the night of June 16, Mildred left the cafeteria after her shift ended at 8:30 p.m. She left with a fellow employee, John McGinnis. They were out on their first date together. McGinnis was a student at Bradley Polytechnic Institute and worked part-time at Bishop's as a busboy. The couple had plans to see the film *The People's Enemy* at the Rialto Theater at 9:00 p.m. McGinnis later testified that Mildred tried to telephone her parents about her plans but could not get an answer.

It was a wet, rainy night and the couple hurried up Jefferson Street to get to the theater. After the film ended, Mildred again tried to call her parents and let them know where she was, but again, could not reach them. The couple left the theater at 11:00 p.m. and tried to catch a country club streetcar at the corner of Main and Jefferson Streets. They missed this car and boarded a different streetcar at the corner of Main and Perry Streets at 11:15 p.m. The couple then got out at Knoxville and Pennsylvania Avenues. McGinnis caught a streetcar back downtown, leaving Mildred to wait for a Peoria Heights streetcar that would take her home.

He waved as he climbed onto the car and departed. It was the last time he would ever see Mildred alive.

At some point between 11:30 p.m. and 2:00 a.m. the next morning, Mildred was kidnapped, savagely raped, and murdered. Her nude body was thrown into a ditch at Springdale Cemetery. The white lace dress that she had been wearing was ripped to shreds and was twisted up beneath her body. Her white sandals were lying in the dirty sand of the ditch and a soggy paper bag was found next to her. It contained white yarn, knitting needles, and a partially finished sweater that she had been working on. She was lying on top of her purse, and a diamond ring was still on her finger, making it obvious that her death had nothing to do with robbery.

The ditch where her body was found was along Valley Road—only four blocks from her home.

News quickly spread about the discovery of Mildred's body. Panic swept the area, and women were cautioned to travel in groups and not accept rides from strangers. The entire city mourned the loss of the young girl and "Peoria's Greatest Manhunt," as the newspaper called it, began. Detectives began questioning suspects, including sideshow workers from a traveling carnival, and known "abnormals" and "morons" in the area.

Soon, calls began coming into police headquarters about rapes and assaults by twenty-five-year-old Gerald Thompson. The young women had been afraid to talk until news spread of Mildred's death. The tips led to the arrest of the young, athletic, and good-looking man. He was a popular, well-liked employee at the Caterpillar tractor plant in East Peoria. He worked there with John Hallmark, Mildred's father, and had even contributed to the flower fund for the girl's funeral. He seemed an unlikely killer, but investigators couldn't ignore the evidence that was piling up against him.

Thompson was arrested on June 21. He confessed two days later. He told police that he had committed at least a dozen assaults and that Springdale

Cemetery was his favorite place to rape women. He usually picked up married women, he said, because they put up more of a fight and that excited him. He kept a list of his attacks in a small black book. He was able to keep the women from reporting him through blackmail. After he raped them, he forced them to stand naked in front of the headlights of his car and then he took photographs of them. If they threatened to report him to the police, he promised to expose them to their husbands and claim they had been willing adulterers. The threats were surprisingly effective, and Thompson got away with it for years. The photographs were later discovered in his home.

A few days later, Thompson tried to withdraw his confession, but it was too late. His trial started just six days after the murder. A crowd formed outside the courthouse doors in Peoria hours before it began. In addition to the usual courtroom seats, benches were provided to fit the maximum number of people into the courtroom. On the second day of the trial, there was a mad scramble for seats in the courtroom and a stampede of women pulled the hinges off the courthouse doors. Several people were knocked down and trampled, but no one was seriously injured.

Along with the spectators were the reporters, jostling for a look at the killer. They came from all over Illinois, from Chicago, and even *Life* magazine sent a reporter and photographer to cover the trial.

The prosecution put on a straightforward case, calling Mildred's sister, Ruth, the Deputy Coroner, and detectives who admitted the clothing that Mildred was wearing that night into evidence. This had a shocking effect on the audience in the courtroom. Many craned their necks to get a glimpse of the torn clothing that told the story of Mildred's final hours.

In his defense, Thompson's court-appointed attorney, Ren Thurman, offered psychiatrists who claimed that Thompson was "sexually insane." He also called a girlfriend who testified that Thompson had always been a perfect gentleman. He did not smoke, drink liquor, or use profanity in her presence.

The jury didn't buy it and quickly returned with a verdict of first-degree murder.

Thompson was sentenced to death and despite appeals to the Illinois Supreme Court and the governor, his execution was scheduled for October 15, 1935. After a last meal of fried chicken and black walnut ice cream, he went to the electric chair. There were 200 spectators to witness his final breath. It was so crowded that those in the front were ordered to get on their knees so that the people in the back could see. Mildred's father, John Hallmark, was forced to stand on a chair to watch.

Two minutes after electricity jolted through his body, Thompson was dead. The tragedy of Mildred Hallmark's murder was finally over—but the story of the "Lady in White" was just beginning.

Ever since Mildred Hallmark's death, there have been reported sightings of a woman in white who roams the grounds of Springdale Cemetery. This ethereal figure is often seen in the vicinity of the Lightner monument, which is close to the spot where Mildred's body was found. She drifts across the grounds, giving off an unearthly light, and then she vanishes.

The woman in the white dress never speaks, but those who are familiar with the terrible murder that took place in the cemetery are convinced of her identity. Her presence alone is enough to remind us of her short life, and violent death, and the fact that she still walks the earth tells a cruel story of a young woman whose existence ended much too soon.

CHICAGO

The only thing that keeps Chicago from being the greatest city in America is the weather. There seems to be something about blizzards and below-zero windchills that tend to put a damper on people's enthusiasm. But whatever Chicago might lack in this regard, it more than makes up for it with its history, legends, and lore—and especially its ghosts!

There are a number of American cities that make the claim of being most haunted, but in my opinion, Chicago leads the pack. There is simply no other city that can boast the sheer number of haunts that Chicago has. The spirits here are simply a part of the city's culture and can be connected to its long and often bloody history. The history and the hauntings of the city go hand in hand. It has often been said that the events of the past create the hauntings of today. In no place is such a statement as true as it is in Chicago, Illinois.

Chicago was a city that was born in blood, as the first settlers here were slaughtered by Native Americans during the Fort Dearborn Massacre. The city was nearly wiped out by the great fire in 1871, and during the early part of the twentieth century, Chicago became synonymous with bootlegging, murder, and gangland violence.

Is it any wonder that the city is so infested with ghosts?

THE ST. VALENTINE'S DAY MASSACRE

Perhaps the most famous event to occur in the history of Chicago crime took place on St. Valentine's Day of 1929, when mob boss Al Capone attempted to wipe out his competition for the rights to control all of the liquor in the city. While this bloody event marked the end of any significant gang opposition to Capone, it was also the act that finally began the decline of his criminal empire.

The bloody events of February 14, 1929, began nearly five years before, with the murder of Dion O'Banion, the leader of Chicago's North Side mob. At that time, control of bootleg liquor in the city raged back and forth between the North Siders, run by O'Banion, and the South Side Outfit, which was controlled by Johnny Torrio and his henchman, Al Capone. In November 1924, Torrio ordered the assassination of O'Banion and started an all-out war in the city. The North Siders retaliated soon afterward and nearly killed Torrio outside his home. This brush with death led to his leaving the city and turning over operations to Capone, who was almost killed in September 1926. The following month, Capone shooters assassinated Hymie Weiss, who had been running the North Side mob after the death of O'Banion. His murder left the operation in the hands of George "Bugs" Moran, a longtime enemy of Capone. For the most part, Moran stood alone against the Capone mob, since most of his allies had succumbed in the fighting. He continued to taunt his powerful enemy and looked for ways to destroy him.

In early 1929, Moran sided with Joe Aiello in another attack against Capone. He and Aiello reportedly gunned down Pasquillano Lolordo, one of Capone's men, and Capone vowed that he would have Moran wiped out on February 14. Capone was living on his estate outside Miami at the time and put in a call to Chicago. He had a very special "valentine" that he wanted delivered to Moran.

Through a contact in Detroit, Capone arranged for someone to call Moran and tell him that a special shipment of hijacked whiskey was going to be delivered to one of Moran's garages on the North Side. Adam Heyer, a friend of Moran's, owned the garage, which was used as a distribution point for North Side liquor. A sign on the front of the building at 2122 North Clark Street read "S-M-C Cartage Co. Shipping—Packing—Long Distance Hauling." Moran received the call at the garage on the morning of February 13, and he arranged to be there to meet the truck the next day.

On the morning of February 14, a group of Moran's men gathered at the Clark Street garage. One of the men was Johnny May, an ex-safecracker who had been hired by Moran as an auto mechanic. He was working on a truck that morning, with his dog, a German shepherd named Highball, tied to the bumper. In addition, waiting for the truck of hijacked whiskey to arrive were six other men: Frank and Pete Gusenberg, who were supposed to meet Moran and pick up two empty trucks to drive to Detroit and pick up smuggled Canadian whiskey; James Clark, Moran's brother-in-law; Adam Heyer; Al Weinshank; and Reinhardt Schwimmer, a young optometrist who had befriended Moran and hung around the liquor warehouse just for the thrill of rubbing shoulders with gangsters.

Bugs Moran was already late for the morning meeting. He was due to arrive at 10:30 but didn't even leave for the rendezvous, in the company of Willie Marks and Ted Newberry, until several minutes after that.

As the seven men waited inside the warehouse, they had no idea that a police car had pulled up outside, or that Moran had spotted the car as he was driving south on Clark Street and, rather than deal with what he believed was a shakedown, stopped at the next corner for a cup of coffee.

Five men got out of the police car, two of them in uniforms and three in civilian clothing. They entered the building, and a few moments later, the clatter of machine-gun fire broke the stillness of the snowy morning. Soon after, five figures emerged and drove away. May's dog, inside the warehouse, began barking and howling.

The landlady in the next building, Jeanette Landesman, was bothered by the sound of the dog and sent one of her boarders, C. L. McAllister, to the garage to see what was going on. He came outside two minutes later, his face a pale white. He ran frantically up the stairs to beg Mrs. Landesman to call the police. The garage was full of dead men!

The police were quickly summoned, and on entering the garage, they were stunned by the carnage. Moran's men had been lined up against the rear wall of the garage and sprayed with machine-gun fire. Pete Gusenberg had died kneeling, slumped over a chair. James Clark had fallen on his face, with half of his head blown away, and Heyer, Schwimmer, Weinshank, and May were thrown lifeless onto their backs. Only one of the men had survived the slaughter, but he lived for only a few hours. Frank Gusenberg had crawled from the blood-sprayed wall where he had fallen and dragged himself into the middle of the dirty floor. He was rushed to the Alexian Brothers Hospital, barely hanging on. Police Sergeant Clarence Sweeney, who had grown up on the same street as Gusenberg, leaned down close to Frank and asked who had shot him.

"No one—nobody shot me," he groaned, and he died later that night.

The death toll of the massacre stood at seven, but the killers had missed Moran. When the police contacted him later and told him what had happened at the garage, he "raved like a madman." To the newspapers, Moran targeted Capone as having ordered the hit. The authorities claimed to be baffled, though, since Capone was in Florida at the time of the massacre. When he was asked to comment on the news, Capone stated, "The only man who kills like that is Bugs Moran." At the same time, Moran was proclaiming, "Only Capone kills guys like that."

And Moran was undoubtedly right. The murders broke the power of the North Side gang, and while there have been many claims as to who the actual shooters were that day, most likely they included John Scalise, Albert Anselmi, and "Machine Gun" Jack McGurn, some of Capone's most trusted men. All three men, along with Joseph Guinta, were arrested, but McGurn had an alibi, and Scalise and Guinta were killed before they could be tried.

The St. Valentine's Day Massacre marked the end of any significant gang opposition to Capone, but it was also the act that finally began the decline of Capone's criminal empire. He had just gone too far, and the authorities, and even Capone's adoring public, were ready to put an end to the bootleg wars.

Chicago, in its own way, memorialized the warehouse on Clark Street where the massacre took place. It became a tourist attraction, and the newspapers even printed the photos of the corpses upside down so that readers would not have to turn their papers around to identify the bodies.

In 1949, the front portion of the S-M-C garage was turned into an antique furniture storage business by a couple who had no idea of the building's bloody past. They soon found that the place was visited much more by tourists, curiosity seekers, and crime buffs than by customers, and they eventually closed the business.

In 1967, the building was demolished. Strangely, bricks that were sold or removed from the site were rumored to be cursed in some way, perhaps affected by the dark and bloody events that occurred in the building.

Whether or not the bricks were somehow haunted by what happened, the site on Clark Street seems to be. Even today people walking along the street at night have reported the sounds of screams and machine guns as they pass the site. The building is long gone now, demolished in some misguided attempt by city officials to erase all vestiges of Chicago's gangster past. A portion of the block was taken over by the Chicago Housing Authority, and now the area where the garage once stood is marked by a fenced-in lawn that belongs to a senior citizens development. Five trees are scattered about the area, and the one in the center marks the point where the rear wall once stood—where Moran's men were lined up and gunned down.

Passersby and the curious have sometimes reported strange sounds, like weeping and moaning, and the indescribable feeling of fear as they walk past. And people accompanied by their dogs have said that the animals seemed to be especially bothered by this spot, sometimes barking and howling, sometimes whining in fear. Their sense of what happened here many years ago seems to be much greater than our own.

Even after all these years, the violent events of the city's gangster era still reverberate over time. Men like Al Capone have left an indelible mark on Chicago, and it appears that the events of St. Valentine's Day 1929 have left one too!

THE SHOW DID NOT GO ON

Perhaps the greatest and most devastating fire in American history occurred in Illinois in October 1871. Known as the Great Chicago Fire, it wiped out most of the old city, killed hundreds, and left hundreds of thousands homeless and destitute. But the city of Chicago has known many tragedies over the years, and this would not be the last of the horrific fires to claim lives in the Windy City.

Another terrible blaze occurred in the crowded Iroquois Theater on December 30, 1903, as a fire broke out during a performance of a vaudeville show starring the popular comedian Eddie Foy. The fire claimed the lives of hundreds of people, including children, who were packed into an afternoon show.

The Iroquois Theater was much acclaimed even before it opened. It was a beautiful place with an ornate lobby, grand staircases, and a front facade that resembled a Greek temple with massive columns. Touted as being "absolutely fireproof," the theater was designed to be safe. It had twenty-five exits that, it was claimed, could empty the building in less than five minutes. The stage had also been fitted with an asbestos curtain that could be quickly lowered to protect the audience.

Though all of this was impressive, it was not enough to battle the real problems that existed with the Iroquois. Seats in the theater were wooden and stuffed with hemp, and much of the precautionary fire equipment that was advertised as having been installed never actually made it into the building. The theater had no fire alarms, and in a rush to open it on time, other safety factors had been forgotten or simply ignored.

The horrific events began on a bitterly cold December day. A holiday crowd had packed into the theater that Wednesday afternoon to see a matinee performance of the hit comedy Mr. Bluebeard.

Around the beginning of the second act, stagehands noticed a spark descend from an overhead light, and then watched some scraps of burning paper fall down onto the stage. In moments, flames began licking at the red velvet curtain. A collective gasp went up from the audience, but no one rushed for the exits. It's believed that the audience merely thought the fire was part of the show.

A few moments later, a flaming set crashed down onto the stage, leaving little doubt that something had gone wrong. A stagehand attempted to lower the asbestos curtain that would protect the audience, but it snagged halfway down, sending a wall of flame out into the audience.

Actors onstage panicked and ran for the doors. Chaos filled the auditorium as the audience began rushing for the theater's Randolph Street entrance. With children in tow, the crowd immediately clogged the gallery and upper balconies. The aisles had become impassable, and as the lights went out, people milled about in blind terror. The auditorium began to fill with heat and smoke, and screams echoed off the walls and ceilings. Through it all, the mass continued to move forward, but when those in front reached the doors, they could not open them. The doors had been designed to swing inward rather than outward, and the crush of people prevented them from opening the doors. Many of those who died not only burned, but also suffocated from the smoke and the crush of bodies. Later, as the police removed the charred remains from the theater, they discovered that a number of victims had been trampled in the panic. One dead woman's face even bore the mark of a shoe heel.

Backstage, theater employees and cast members opened a rear set of double doors, which sucked the wind inside and caused flames to fan out under the asbestos curtain and into the auditorium. A second gust of wind created a fireball that shot into the galleries and balconies filled with people. All of the stage drops were now on fire, and as they burned, they engulfed the supposedly noncombustible asbestos curtain, which collapsed and plunged into the seats of the theater.

The fire burned for almost fifteen minutes before an alarm was raised at a box down the street. From outside, there appeared to be nothing wrong. It was so quiet that the first firefighters to arrive thought it was a false alarm.

This changed when they tried to open the auditorium doors and found they could not—too many bodies were stacked up against them. They were able to gain access only by pulling the bodies out of the way with pike poles, peeling them off one another, and then climbing over the stacks of corpses. It took just ten minutes to put out the blaze, as the intense heat inside had already eaten up anything that would still burn. The firefighters made their way into the blackened auditorium and were met with only silence and smell of death. They called out for survivors, but no one answered their cry.

The gallery and upper balconies sustained the greatest loss of life, as the patrons had been trapped by locked doors at the top of the stairways. The firefighters found 200 bodies stacked there, as many as 10 deep. Those who escaped had ripped the metal bars from the front of the balcony and jumped onto the crowds below. Even then, most of these met their death at a lower level.

A few who made it to the fire escape door behind the top balcony found that the iron staircase was missing. In its place was a platform with a plunge of about a hundred feet to the cobblestone alley below. Across the alley, behind the theater, painters were working on a building occupied by Northwestern University's dental school. When they realized what was happening at the theater, they quickly erected a makeshift bridge using ladders and wooden planks, which they extended across the alley to the fire escape platform. Reports vary as to how many they saved, but several people managed to climb across the bridge to safety. Others plunged to their death as they tried to escape across the ladder, and many times that number jumped from the ledge or were pushed by the milling crowd that pressed through the doors behind them. The passageway behind the theater is still referred to as "Death Alley" today, after nearly 150 victims were found here.

When it was all over, 572 people had died in the fire and more died later, bringing the eventual death toll up to 602, including 212 children. For nearly five hours, police officers, firemen, and even newspaper reporters carried out the dead. Anxious relatives sifted through the remains, searching for loved ones. Other bodies were taken away by police wagons and ambulances and transported to a temporary morgue at Marshall Field's on State Street. Medical examiners and investigators worked all through the night.

The city went into mourning. Newspapers carried lists and photographs of the dead, and the mayor banned all New Year's celebrations. An investigation into the fire brought to light a number of troubling facts. The supposedly fireproof "asbestos" curtain was really made from cotton and other combustible materials. It never would have saved anyone at all. There were no fire alarms in the building, and the owners had decided that sprinklers were too unsightly and costly and never had them installed.

To make matters worse, the management also established an unsafe policy to keep nonpaying customers from slipping into the theater during a performance: They quietly bolted nine pairs of iron panels over the rear doors and installed padlocked, accordion-style gates at the top of the interior second- and third-floor stairway landings. And just as tragic was the idea they had come up with to keep the audience from being distracted during a show: They had ordered all of the exit lights to be turned off.

The investigation led to a cover-up by officials from the city and the fire department, who denied all knowledge of fire code violations. They blamed the inspectors, who had overlooked the problems in exchange for free theater passes. A grand jury indicted a number of individuals, including the theater owners, fire officials, and even the mayor, but no one was ever charged with a criminal act. Families of the dead filed nearly 275 civil lawsuits against the theater, but no money was ever collected.

The Iroquois Theater Fire ranks as the nation's fourth-deadliest blaze and the deadliest single-building fire in American history. Nevertheless, the building was repaired and reopened briefly in 1904 as Hyde and Behmann's Music Hall, and then in 1905 as the Colonial Theater. In 1924, the building was razed to make room for a new theater, the Oriental, but the facade of the Iroquois was used in its construction. The Oriental operated at what is now 24 West Randolph Street until the middle part of 1981, when it fell into disrepair and was closed down. It opened again as a wholesale electronics dealership for a time, but then went dark again. The restored theater is now part of the Civic Tower Building and is next door to the restored Delaware Building. It reopened as the Ford Center for the Performing Arts in 1998.

But this has not stopped the tales of the old Iroquois Theater from being told, especially in light of more recent—and more ghostly—events. People who live and work in this area report that "Death Alley" is not as empty as it appears to be. The narrow passageway that runs behind the theater is rarely used today, except for the occasional delivery truck or a lone pedestrian who is in a hurry to get somewhere else. It is largely deserted, but why? The stories say that those few who do pass through the alley often find themselves very uncomfortable and unsettled here. They say that faint cries are sometimes heard in the shadows and that some have reported being touched by unseen hands and feeling eerie cold spots that seem to come from nowhere and vanish just as quickly.

Could the alleyway and the surrounding area actually be haunted? Do the spirits of those who met their tragic end inside the burning theater still linger here?

GHOSTS OF THE EASTLAND DISASTER

One of the most devastating—and haunting—tragedies to strike Chicago was the capsizing of the *Eastland* steamer on July 24, 1915, between the Clark and LaSalle Street Bridges. The horrific accident not only claimed the lives of scores of people but also left behind an impression that still resonates in downtown Chicago today.

Eastland was just one of several steamships that had been contracted by the Western Electric company to take its employees and families to Michigan City, Indiana, for the annual summer picnic. *Eastland*, which had a reputation for being top-heavy, was moored on the south side of the Chicago River, and after the passengers were loaded onboard, the dock lines were loosed, and the ship prepared to depart. Because it was overcrowded, the crew had released some of the ballast, which made it ride higher on the river. This would turn out to be a disastrous idea.

The overflow crowd, dressed in their best summer attire even on this drizzly morning, jammed onto the decks, waving handkerchiefs and calling out to those still onshore. The ship eased away from the dock and immediately began to list to one side. As more passengers pushed toward that side of the deck, the boat tilted dangerously.

The passengers on deck were thrown into the water, and the river became a moving sea of bodies. Crews on the other boats threw life preservers into the river, while onlookers began throwing lines, boxes, and anything else that would float to the floundering passengers. The river was now surging, thanks to the wake caused by the overturned ship, and many of the luckless passengers were pulled beneath the water by the current or swamped by the crashing waves.

A more dire fate awaited those passengers who had remained inside the ship. These unlucky victims were first thrown to one side of the ship as it turned over, and then covered with water as the river rushed inside. A few of them managed to escape to the upturned end of the ship, but most didn't, becoming trapped in a tangled heap at the lowest point of Eastland.

Firefighters and rescue workers arrived within minutes and began cutting holes in the wood above the waterline and in the steel hull below it. In the first fateful minutes, a number of passengers managed to escape, but soon it was simply too late. The rescue workers had to resign themselves to fishing corpses out of the water, which they wrapped in sheets and transferred to the Roosevelt, another vessel that had been rented for the excursion. The big downtown stores sent wagons and trucks to ferry the injured and dead to nearby hospitals and makeshift morgues. Large grappling hooks were also used to pull bodies from the water. By late that afternoon, nearly 200 bodies had been taken to a nearby National Guard Armory, which was used as a temporary morgue. By the time it was all over, 835 of the ship's passengers had perished, including 22 entire families. It was one of the most tragic days in Chicago history, but the story did not end there.

The first bodies that were recovered on the day of the tragedy were taken to the nearby Reid-Murdoch Building, where Chicago's traffic court is now located, or to local mortuaries. The only public building nearby that was large enough to serve as a morgue was the 2nd Illinois Regiment National Guard Armory on Carpenter Street, between Randolph and Washington. The bodies were carried into the building, one after another, for hours. They were laid out in rows of eighty-five and assigned numbers. Any personal possessions that came in with them were placed in envelopes, each of which was marked with the corresponding number of the corpse. Loved ones and family members searched through the rows in search of familiar faces. The cries and wails of the bereaved echoed off the walls of the armory for days, and the Red Cross treated thirty women for exhaustion and hysteria during the ordeal. The last of the bodies was identified on Friday, July 30.

As the years passed, so did the need for an armory so close to downtown Chicago. The military closed it and sold off the building, which was used a number of times over the years as a stable and a bowling alley. Years later, the armory building became part of Harpo Studios, the production company owned by Oprah Winfrey.

But the success that the show brought to the old armory building was able to put to rest the spirits of the *Eastland* disaster. Many who worked there claimed that the ghosts of the perished passengers were still restless in the new studios. Employees reported many strange encounters that could be explained, including the sighting of an apparition that was dubbed the Gray Lady. In addition, staff members heard whispering voices, the laughter of children, sobbing sounds, old-time music, the clinking of phantom glasses, and the tapping of invisible footsteps, frequently heard on the lobby staircase. Doors near the staircase often slammed shut without assistance. Many staff members believed it to be a very haunted place.

Harpo Studios is gone now. The old armory was torn down and replaced by new building from which no new stories of the old ghosts have emerged. Even so, the spirits of *Eastland* do not rest in peace.

At the site of the disaster, there are still reports of cries of terror being heard from the river. For many years, passersby on the Clark Street Bridge have claimed to hear shouts and moans coming from the water, along with blood-curdling screams. There are also numerous reports of people who appear to be drowning in the river but when rescuers attempt to help, the victims simply vanish.

A historical plaque now marks the place where the disaster occurred, but it is not the only reminder that hundreds of people died at this spot. The ghosts of the past serve as a reminder, too.

HAUNTED BACHELOR'S GROVE CEMETERY

Located southwest of Chicago is the Rubio Woods Forest Preserve, an island of trees and shadows nestled in the urban sprawl of the area. On the edge of the forest is a small graveyard that many believe may be the most haunted place in the region. The name of this cemetery is Bachelor's Grove, and this ramshackle burial ground may be infested with more ghosts than most can imagine. Over the years, the place has been cursed with more than 100 documented reports of paranormal phenomena, from actual apparitions to glowing balls of light.

There have been no new burials here for many years, and it likely doesn't provide much peace for the departed buried within its borders. It is a place that has seen chaos, destruction, midnight trespassers and an unusually large number of spirits.

The history of Bachelor's Grove is a confusing one, but most historians believe that it was started at some point in the 1830s. The name—sometimes spelled "Batchelor"—originally seems to have come from a settlement near the future cemetery, which was founded in the 1820s. It consisted of mostly German immigrants who had moved west from New York, Vermont, and Connecticut. The village remained Batchelor's Grove for some years, but then in 1850, its name was changed to "Bremen" by postmaster Samuel Everden, in honor of the city in Germany. In 1855, it was changed back by Postmaster Robert Patrick, but the post office closed just three years later.

The cemetery itself has a much stranger history—or at least a more mysterious one. The land was purchased from the government by the Everden family in 1835, but some reports claim that the section that would soon become an official cemetery already had burials on it when the Everdens bought the property. Whether this is true or not, the land was designated as a burial ground in 1844, and the first recorded burial was that of Eliza (Mrs. Leonard H.) Scott. At that time, it was known as Everden Cemetery after the family that owned the property.

The last caretaker of the cemetery was a man named Clarence Fulton, whose family were early settlers in the township. By that time, the nearby settlements were gone. The land where homes and businesses had stood was now part of the Cook County Forest Preserve—and so was the cemetery and the nearby quarry pond. The quarry had been started by Christ Boehm in 1909, and it operated until the 1920s when it was closed by Forest Preserve District. By the time the forest preserve took over the area, there were very few people living nearby.

Even so, it was a popular recreation area. The Midlothian Country Club was a short distance away, and in the 1930s it was a common practice for young people to meet at a local dance hall and picnic area and walk over to the cemetery to "get scared." At that time, Bachelor's Grove was described as "serene" and "undisturbed." And that was even after the attention that the graveyard gained in April 1934, when readers of Robert L. Ripley's "Believe It or Not" newspaper column featured Bachelor's Grove for its name and the ironic fact that women were still buried there.

But the peaceful atmosphere of the cemetery was soon to come to an end. By the early 1950s, the first problems began to be reported. Just a few years before, the nearby turnpike had been scheduled to be abandoned, leading to fewer people who passed by the graveyard regularly. Its isolated setting helped the gravel drive that passed the cemetery become a popular "lover's lane." Vandals followed.

On September 11, 1952, the first newspaper reports of vandalism at Bachelor's Grove noted that "at least 10 granite monument headstones" had been knocked over by vandals. Things became so bad that police officers had to make daily visits to the cemetery to keep visitors away.

More damage was reported in April 1958, when several smaller tombstones were pulled out of the ground. In 1965, coffins were unearthed, and at least one was burned. More tombstones were knocked over, sprayed with paint, broken apart, and even stolen. In 1973, another coffin was exhumed, although the vandals were captured by the police.

Year after year, reports appeared in the newspapers that included shocking photos of desecrated stones, opened graves, bones that are strewn about, and of course, ghosts. The 1970s marked the first time that Bachelor's Grove was being designated as "one of the most haunted places in America." Though ghost stories had been told locally about the burial ground for at least two decades by the time of the first publicized desecrations, they were now reaching a much wider audience.

Which came first—the destruction or the hauntings? There was no doubt that Bachelor's Grove was a spooky spot as early as the 1930s. If it hadn't been, it never would have become a so-called lover's lane, and young men wouldn't have been taking their girlfriends there from the local dance hall to scare them.

But it seems that things became worse—and much more frightening—after the vandals began wreaking havoc on the cemetery grounds. It appeared that the vandalism had "stirred something up" at Bachelor's Grove, and most researchers have come to believe that this might be the source of the haunting activity.

But others will swear the cemetery is haunted for another reason. Starting in the late 1970s, forest rangers and cemetery visitors began making grim discoveries within the fence that surrounded the burial ground. It was not uncommon to stumble across the remains of chickens, cats, and other small animals that appeared to have been mutilated in a ritualistic fashion. Officers who have patrolled the surrounding woods at night have reported seeing evidence of black magic and occult rituals in and around the graveyard. In some cases, inscriptions and elaborate writings have been carved into and painted on trees, on grave markers, and the cemetery earth. This has led many to believe that the cemetery has been used for occult activities. If that didn't cause the cemetery to become haunted, it may have made things worse.

A visit to Bachelor's Grove today does little to convince anyone that it was once a "peaceful and serene" place. It is overgrown with weeds and surrounded by a high, chain-link fence but is easily accessible, thanks to the holes that have been cut in it by trespassers. The cemetery sign that was once above the entrance has been gone for years.

The first thing that a visitor will notice is the destruction. Tombstones seem almost randomly placed, many no longer marking the resting places of those whose names are carved upon them. Many of the stones are missing, lost forever. The missing markers gave birth to legends about how the stones of the cemetery move about under their own power. They don't. They have simply been knocked over by vandals or carried away by thieves.

Even more disturbing than the missing and toppled stones are the unfinished exhumations of graves, where vandals have attempted to disturb the bodies of the dead.

Just past the back edge of the cemetery is the small, stagnant pond, left behind when the quarry closed in 1927. Years before, rumors claimed that gangsters from Chicago dumped the bodies of murder victims in the secluded pond. There are no news reports to substantiate the stories, but the violence of the era didn't leave the local vicinity untouched. Local newspapers were filled with stories of the explosion of homemade liquor stills, raids on the operators of the stills, and bullet-riddled bodies of rivals found dumped along desolate area roads.

On October 21, 1927, a local bootlegger named Fred Passini had been taken on a "one-way ride" and his body was tossed into a ditch just a few blocks away from Bachelor's Grove. He had been shot in the head nine times. The following summer, a farmer and his son found an identified man not far from the cemetery. He had been shot in the head and tossed from a moving car. With these murder victims found so nearby, it makes the chances that bodies were dumped in the quarry pond even greater. Perhaps their spirits have also lingered behind.

But those aren't the strangest things connected to the pond.

One night in the late 1970s, two Cook County Forest Preserve officers were on night patrol near the cemetery and claimed to see the apparition of a horse emerge from the waters of the pond. The animal appeared to be pulling a plow behind it that was steered by the ghost of an older man. The two apparitions crossed the road in front of the rangers' vehicle—were clearly visible for a moment in the glare of their headlights—and then vanished into the woods. The men simply stared in shock for a moment and then looked at one another to be sure that they had both seen the same thing. They later reported the incident—as would others in years to come.

The sightings of the farmer and his horse have given birth to a legend that may explain the encounters. The story goes that a farmer was plowing a nearby field in the 1870s, and his horse was spooked by something. The farmer became tangled in the reins and was dragged behind the horse into the pond. Unable to free himself, he was pulled down into the murky water by the weight of the horse and the plow, and he drowned.

Of course, you may have noticed a small problem with this legend since the pond didn't exist until it was dug by Christ Boehm's quarry operation in 1909. So, while the story may not be true, there is still no way to explain the credible sightings of the farmer and the horse. They remain yet another of the mysteries of Bachelor's Grove.

If you go searching for Bachelor's Grove Cemetery, it's recommended that you don't go at night. There are more than ghosts lurking in the surrounding woods—like Forest Preserve officers who will write you a ticket for trespassing or may even take you to jail. The protection of the cemetery is taken very seriously.

But if you do go—during the daytime, of course—you'll find the cemetery by leaving the road and walking up an overgrown gravel path into the woods. The old road is blocked with concrete barriers to prevent anyone from driving on it, and a dented "no trespassing" sign hangs across it on a rusted chain. The burial ground lies about a half-mile or so beyond it in the woods.

And yes, even the trail is haunted.

It's from the trail where most of the reports of "ghost lights" come from. They've been seen by literally hundreds of people over the years and are white, flicking lights that are larger than fireflies and move very quickly and erratically. There is a report of a red, beacon-like light, too. It flies rapidly back and forth along the path to the cemetery. It's said to be so bright and so fast that it's impossible to tell what it looks like. Most witnesses state that they have seen a "red streak" that it has left in its wake.

It's along this deserted road where other strange events connected to the cemetery are reported. Perhaps the strangest is the numerous sightings of the "phantom house." It has been seen along the trail for several decades—appearing and disappearing—often by people who had no idea that no house was supposed to be there.

The house along the trail has been reported in all weather conditions, in the daytime and at night. There is no historical record of a house ever existing near the cemetery, but the descriptions of it rarely vary. Each person claims it to be an older two-story farmhouse, painted white, with wooden posts, a porch swing, and a welcoming light that burns softly in the window. No one has ever claimed to have set foot on that front porch—and perhaps that's for the best because it has a nasty habit of vanishing. It's merely there one moment—looking completely solid, stable, and life-like—and then it's gone as if it never existed at all.

To make matters more confusing, the house has been seen at dozens of different locations around the cemetery. Rarely is it reported in the same place twice. There is no explanation for it, and sightings of the house further add to the chilling ambience of Bachelor's Grove.

There have been many sightings of ghosts and phantoms within the cemetery itself over the years. They run the gamut from reports of figures in dark robes to a man in a yellow suit, a tall, shadowy figure, women in mourning clothes, and much more. But there is no spirit encountered as frequently as the woman who has been called everything from the "Madonna of Bachelor's Grove" to the "White Lady" to the affectionate "Mrs. Rogers."

The stories say that she is the ghost of a woman who was buried in the cemetery next to the grave of her young child. She reportedly wanders the cemetery at night with an infant wrapped in her arms. She walks aimlessly, completely unaware of those who claim they have seen her.

There have been many reports from those who claim to have seen her, but no clear evidence as to who she might have been in life. There are several possible candidates. One of them is Amelia Patrick, the first wife of Senator John Humphrey. Their infant daughter, Libby May, died and was buried with Amelia's family at Bachelor's Grove, although Amelia was later buried elsewhere. Could her spirit have come to Bachelor's Grove to search for her child?

There are also two sisters-in-law who could be the "White Lady"—Katherine Fulton and Luella Rogers. Katherine, who married Luella's brother Bert Fulton, was heartbroken by the death of her daughter, Marci May, who died in infancy. The baby was buried at the Fulton family plot in Bachelor's Grove. Katherine, like Amelia Patrick, was buried elsewhere after she died, and it's suggested that perhaps her spirit could also be searching for her child.

Luella Rogers was killed by a hit-and-run driver in 1937 and buried at Bachelor's Grove, also in the Fulton family plot. Luella's baby sister, Emma, is buried with her in the same plot, but her grave marker was stolen long ago. It was later recovered, but it was not returned to the cemetery. Instead, it was placed in the care of the Tinley Park Historical Society. Some believe that Luella's spirit is upset by her sister's missing stone, and that might be what she is looking for as she wanders the grounds of Bachelor's Grove.

Countless people have had experiences in this cemetery that they cannot explain and there is little doubt that it is a very strange place. Is it as haunted as so many believe? And if so, is the haunting caused by the desecration that the burial ground has endured over the years? That's something you'll have to decide for yourself and perhaps you, like so many others, will come to believe that it is one of the most haunted places in the Illinois.

THE ITALIAN BRIDE

In Hillside, Illinois, just outside of Chicago, is Mount Carmel Cemetery. In addition to being the final resting place of Al Capone, Dion O'Banion, and other notorious Chicago mobsters, the cemetery is also the burial place of a woman named Julia Buccola Petta.

While her name may not spring to mind as a part of Illinois history, for those intrigued by the supernatural, she is better known as the "Italian Bride." Julia's grave is marked today by a life-sized statue of the unfortunate woman in her wedding dress, a stone reproduction of the wedding photo that is mounted on the front of her monument. While a beautiful monument, there is nothing about it to suggest that anything weird ever occurred in connection to it. However, once you know the history behind the site, it's soon realized that this is one of the weirdest tales in the annals of American graveyards.

Julia was born on June 6, 1891, in Italy. Her father, George, died in 1913, and her mother, Filomena, emigrated to the United States with her daughter. They traveled to the west side of Chicago, where three other Buccola children— Henry, Joseph, and Rosalia—were already settled. In June 1920, Julia married Matthew Petta at Holy Rosary Church on North Damen Avenue. Julia became pregnant soon after the wedding, but complications occurred, and on March 17, 1921, Julia died while giving birth to her son, Filippo. Because of the Italian tradition that dying in childbirth made the woman a type of martyr, Julia was buried in white, the martyrs' color. Her wedding dress also served as her burial gown, and with her dead infant tucked into her arms, the two were laid to rest in a single coffin at Mount Carmel Cemetery.

Filomena Buccola was inconsolable over her daughter's death. Shortly after Julia was buried, Filomena began to experience strange and terrifying dreams every night. In these nightmares, she envisioned Julia telling her that she was still alive and needed her help. For the next six years, the dreams plagued Filomena, and she began trying, without success, to have her daughter's grave opened, and her body exhumed. She was unable to explain why she needed to do this; she only knew that she should. Finally, through sheer persistence, her request was granted, and a sympathetic judge passed down an order for Julia's exhumation.

In 1927, six years after Julia's death, the casket was finally removed from the grave. When it was opened, Julia's body was found not to have decayed at all. It was said that her flesh was still as soft as it had been when she was alive. A photograph was taken at the time of the exhumation, and it shows Julia's "incorruptible" body in the casket. Filomena set out to raise money for a more elaborate tombstone. The finished work would be a grandiose tribute to her dead daughter—a life-size sculpture of Julia on her wedding day.

Filomena—financed by prayer cards and donations—added the postmortem photo of Julia to the front of her grave monument. Below the image is the Italian phrase *Presa Dopo 6 Anni Morta*, which roughly translates to "taken 6 years after death." A photo of Julia in her bridal gown, the inspiration for the statue, was also fastened to the stone.

The postmortem photograph shows a body that appears to be fresh, with no discoloration of the skin, even after six years. The rotted and decayed appearance of the coffin in the photo, however, bears witness to the fact that it had been underground for some time. Julia appears to be merely sleeping. Her family took the fact that she was found to be so well preserved as a sign from God, and so, after collecting money from other family members and neighbors, they created the impressive monument that stands over her grave today.

What mysterious secret rests at the grave of Julia Petta? How could her body have stayed in perfect condition after lying in the grave for six years?

Many devout Catholics in the neighborhood believed that Julia's "incorruptibility" meant that she was a saint. Skeptics scoffed at the idea, claiming that the postmortem photo must have been taken before she was originally buried—although this doesn't explain the condition of the casket or the decomposition of the infant that is nestled in her arms. Another explanation was attributed to adipocere, also known as "corpse wax"—"a waxy substance consisting chiefly of fatty acids and calcium soaps that is formed during the decomposition of dead body fat in moist or wet anaerobic conditions." In other words, the shape and state of Julia's body were preserved by a natural process.

Of course, these explanations did little to dispel the local belief that Julia's preserved body was proof of a miracle. But was it really? There were stories that have since been told about her mother, Filomena, questioning the reality of her dreams. Some claimed that she fabricated the entire story as retaliation for a marriage of which she did not approve. She never liked Matthew Petta, the stories say, and this claim is given some credence by the fact that Julia's married name does not appear on the grave monument—only Buccola.

But even if Filomena lied about her nightmares to gain sympathy from the community and to help finance the building of the elaborate monument, how does this explain the postmortem photograph? The photo of Julia in her casket—six years after her death—appears to be real. It has defied explanation for nearly a century.

And that's not the end of this odd story. Reports have been told over the years of a ghostly "woman in white" who has been seen wandering at the edge of the cemetery where she rests. Stories claim to have seen her in the daytime and at night, and many who know the story of Julia Petta believe that this is her restless spirit.

One eerie tale that was told involved a young boy who was accidentally left behind at the cemetery, not far from Julia's grave. When his family returned to Mount Carmel to look for him, they saw him holding the hand of a dark-haired young woman in a white dress. When the boy ran toward his parents, the woman in white disappeared.

JANE ADDAMS'S HULL HOUSE

Hull House was constructed by Charles J. Hull at Halsted and Polk Streets in 1856, at a time when this was one of the most fashionable sections of the city. After the Chicago Fire of 1871, the better classes moved to other parts of the city, and the Near West Side began to attract a large immigrant population of Italian, Greek, and Jewish settlers. By the 1880s, Hull House was surrounded by factories and tenement houses, and soon after, it became one of the most famous places in Chicago. Although it was never intended to be known as a haunted house, it would not emerge from its heyday unscathed by stories of ghosts and the supernatural.

Hull House did not achieve its fame as a private home, but rather as a pioneering effort of social equality that was started by a woman named Jane Addams and her friend Ellen Starr Gates. They opened the house in 1889, at time when the overcrowded tenement neighborhoods west of Halsted Street were a jungle of crime, vice, prostitution, and drug addiction. Jane Addams became the "voice of humanity" on the West Side, enriching the lives of many unfortunate people at the house.

Jane Addams was born and raised under pleasant surroundings in the village of Cedarville, the privileged daughter of a wealthy merchant. Tragedy first came into her life with the death of her father, which occurred the same year that she graduated from the Rockford Female Seminary. She went into a deep depression, and unsure what to do with her life, she spent a portion of her inheritance traveling in Europe. It was in London, in the terrible slums of Whitechapel, that she finally found her calling.

In the company of her college friend and traveling companion Ellen Starr Gates, Jane spent time at Toynbee Hall, a settlement house for the poor. Here young and affluent students lived and worked beside the poorest dregs of London, pushing for social reform and better standards of living. Jane was intrigued by the idea, and after her return to Chicago, she began making plans for such a place in the city. She soon discovered the run-down Halsted Street mansion and the terrible neighborhood around it.

Jane and Ellen took control of the property in September 1889 and opened a settlement house. It was to the broken-down refugees and immigrants in the area that Jane Addams's Hull House appealed. Addams was granted a twenty-five-year, rent-free lease by Hull's confidential secretary, Helen Culver, and by the heirs to the Hull fortune, who were enthusiastic about Jane's efforts on behalf of the poor. The two women soon began turning the place into a comfortable house, aimed mostly at women, but affording food and shelter to the homeless and hungry as well. The house also provided education and protection for many, and the staff worked to better the lives of the local people for many years to come.

At the time when Jane Addams took over Hull House, several years had passed since the death of Mrs. Charles Hull, but this apparently didn't prevent her from making her presence known. She had died of natural causes in a second-floor bedroom of the mansion, and within a few months of her passing, her ghost was said to be haunting that particular room. Overnight guests began having their sleep disturbed by footsteps and what they described as strange and unearthly noises.

Mrs. Hull's bedroom was first occupied by Jane, who was awakened one night by loud footsteps in the otherwise empty room. After a few nights of this, she confided her story to Ellen, who also admitted to hearing the same sounds. Jane later moved to another room. Others also experienced the unusual happenings. Helen Campbell, the author of the book *Prisoners of Poverty*, took Jane up on the offer of staying in the "haunted room" and reported seeing an apparition standing next to her bed. When she lit the gas jet, the figure vanished.

According to Jane, earlier tenants of the house had also thought the upstairs of the house was haunted. They had always kept a bucket of water on the stairs, believing that the ghost was unable to cross over it. Unfortunately this was not the only supernatural legend connected to the house.

Hull House received its greatest notoriety when it was alleged to be the refuge of the Chicago Devil Baby. This child supposedly was born to a devout Catholic woman and her atheist husband and was said to have pointed ears, horns, scale-covered skin, and a tail. According to the story, the young woman had attempted to display a picture of the Virgin Mary in the house, but her husband tore it down. He stated that he would rather have the devil himself in the house than that picture. When the woman became pregnant, the Devil Baby had been their curse. After enduring numerous indignities because of the child, the father allegedly took it to Hull House.

Reportedly Jane Addams took in the baby, and staff members of the house took it to be baptized. During the ceremony, the baby supposedly escaped from the priest and began dancing and laughing. Not knowing what else to do with the child, the story goes, Jane kept it locked in the attic of the house, where it later died.

Rumors spread quickly about the baby, and within a few weeks, hundreds of people came to the house to get a glimpse of it. How the story had gotten started no one knew, but it spread throughout the West Side neighborhood and was reported by famous Chicago reporter Ben Hecht. He claimed that every time he tried to run down the story, he was directed to find the child at Hull House. Many people came to the door and demanded to see the child, and others quietly offered to pay an admission.

Each day Jane turned people away and tried to convince them that the story was fabricated. She even devoted forty pages of her autobiography to dispelling the stories. Even though most of the poorly educated immigrants left the house still believing the tales of the Devil Baby, the stream of callers eventually died out, and the story became a barely remembered side note in the history of Hull House. Or did it?

As the years have passed, some people still maintain that the story of the Devil Baby is true—or at least contains some elements of the truth. Some have speculated that perhaps the child was actually a badly deformed infant that had been brought to Hull House by a young immigrant woman that could not care for it. Perhaps the monstrous appearance of the child had started the rumors in the neighborhood and eventually led to Hull House.

Regardless, local legend insists that at some point, a disfigured boy was hidden away on the upper floors of the house. The stories also go on to say that on certain nights, the image of a deformed face could be seen peering out of the attic window, and that a ghostly version of that face is still seen by visitors today.

Hull House has not been a settlement house for many years, but people still come here. They are not just tourists and historians, but ghost hunters too. The eerie stories told by Jane Addams and the occupants of Hull House are still recalled when weird happenings take place in these modern times. It is common for the motion sensors of the alarm system to be mysteriously triggered. When security officers respond, they find that the house is empty, and there is no sign of a break-in or any disturbance. Officers state that no building on the University of Illinois at Chicago campus (which maintains the house) has as many false calls as Hull House does. They have also answered reports about people inside the house or looking out the windows, but the police have never found anyone in the place.

CHICAGO'S VANISHING HITCHHIKERS

Tales of phantom hitchhikers can be found all over the country, but it seems that in no city are they as prevalent as they are in Chicago. A number of mysterious phantoms have been reported here, including vanishing hitchers and what some have dubbed "prophesying passengers," strange hitchhikers who are picked up and then pass along odd messages, usually involving the end of the world or something else dire.

One Chicago story tells of a prophesying nun. A cab driver once told of a strange and unsettling fare that he had picked up in December 1941. He was cruising the downtown streets in his cab one night, and he pulled over to let in a nun who was dressed in the traditional garb of a Catholic order. She gave him the address where she wished to be taken, and they drove off. The radio was on, and the announcer was discussing the events that had taken place at Pearl Harbor a short time before and the preparations that the United States was making for war.

The nun suddenly spoke up from the backseat. "It won't last more than four months," she said, and then didn't speak again for the rest of the ride.

When the cabbie reached the address, he got out to open the door for the sister but was surprised to discover that she wasn't there! Thinking that the little old lady had forgotten to pay her fare, the driver climbed the steps of the address she had given him and found that it was a convent. He knocked on the door and was brought to the Mother Superior. He explained his predicament to her, but she told him that none of the sisters had been downtown that day. She asked the driver what the nun had looked like.

As the driver began to describe her, he happened to look up at a portrait that was hanging on the wall behind the Mother Superior's desk. He pointed to the picture and, in an excited voice, told her that the woman in the portrait was the nun he had brought to the convent house. He probably thought that he was going to get his fare after all—but he couldn't have been more wrong. The Mother Superior smiled and quietly said, "But she has been dead for ten years."

And the nun, like those phantom passengers who tell of the end of the world, was incorrect in her prediction about the short end to World War II. One has to wonder: If these beings are truly supernatural, then perhaps they should consider another source to get their information on upcoming events!

Another passenger from the Windy City had her own strange prediction to make. During Chicago's Century of Progress Exposition in 1933, a group of people in an automobile told of a bizarre encounter. They were traveling along Lake Shore Drive when a woman with a suitcase, standing by the roadside, hailed them. They invited her to ride along with them, and she climbed in. They later said that they never really got a good look at her, because it was dark outside.

As they drove along, they got into a conversation about the exposition, and the mysterious woman oddly told them, "The fair is going to slide off into Lake Michigan in September." She then gave them her address in Chicago and invited them to call on her anytime. When they turn around to speak to her again, after this doom-filled warning, they discovered that she had disappeared.

Unnerved, they decided to go to the address the woman gave them, and when they did, a man answered the door. They explained to him why they had come to the house, and he merely nodded his head and told them, "Yes, that was my wife. She died four years ago."

Another ghostly hitchhiker apparently haunts the roadways between the site of the old Melody Mill Ballroom and Waldheim Cemetery, which is located at 1800 South Harlem Avenue. The cemetery, once known as Jewish Waldheim, is one of the more peaceful and attractive graveyards in the area and is easily recognizable from the columns that are mounted at the front gates. They were once part of the old Cook County Building, which was demolished in 1908. This cemetery would most likely go quietly through its existence if not for the tales of the Flapper Ghost, as the resident spirit has been dubbed.

The story of this beautiful spirit tells of her earthly existence as a young Jewish girl who attended dances at the Melody Mill Ballroom, formerly on Des Plaines Avenue. During its heyday, the ballroom was one of the city's favorite venues for ballroom dancing and played host to dozens of popular big bands from the 1920s to the mid-1980s. The brick building was topped with a miniature windmill, the ballroom's trademark.

This young woman was a very attractive brunette with bobbed hair and a penchant for dressing in the style of the Prohibition era. In later years, witnesses claimed that her ghost dressed like a flapper, and this is how she earned her nickname. Legend has it that this lovely girl was a regular at the Melody Mill until she died of peritonitis, the result of a burst appendix.

The girl was buried at Jewish Waldheim, and she likely would have been forgotten, left to rest in peace, if strange things had not started to happen a few months later. Staff members at the Melody Mill began to see a young woman who looked just like the deceased girl appearing at dances at the ballroom. A number of men actually claimed to have met the girl there, after her death, and offered her a ride home. During the journey, the young woman always vanished. This fetching phantom was also known to hitch rides on Des Plaines Avenue, outside the ballroom, and was sometimes seen near the gates to the cemetery. Some travelers who passed the graveyard claimed to see her entering a mausoleum that was located off Harlem Avenue.

The ghost was most active in 1933, during the Century of Progress Exhibition. She became active again forty years later, during the early 1970s, and stayed active for nearly a decade, although recent sightings have been few.

In the early 1930s, she was often reported at the ballroom, where she would dance with young men and ask for a ride home at the end of the evening. Every report was basically the same. A young man agreed to drive the girl home, and she would give him directions to go east on Cermak Road, then north on Harlem Avenue. When they reached the cemetery, the girl always asked the driver to stop the car. She would explain to them that she lived in the caretaker's house, since demolished, and then get out of the car. One man stated that he watched the girl go toward the house but then duck around the side of it. Curious, he climbed out of the car to see where she was going and saw her run out into the cemetery and vanish among the tombstones.

Another young man, who was also told that the girl lived in the caretaker's house, decided to come back during the day and ask about her at the house. He had become infatuated with her and hoped to take her dancing again another evening. His questions to the occupants of the house were met with blank stares and bafflement. No such girl lived, or had ever lived, at the house.

More sightings took place in the early 1970s, and one report even occurred during the daylight hours. A family visiting the cemetery one day was startled to see a young woman dressed like a flapper walking toward a crypt, where she suddenly disappeared. The family hurried over to the spot, only to find that the girl was not there, and there was nowhere to which she could have vanished so quickly.

Since that time, sightings of the Flapper Ghost have been few, and this may be because the old Melody Mill is no more. The days of jazz and big bands were gone by the 1980s, and attendance on weekend evenings continued to slip, until the place was closed down in 1985. It was later demolished, and a new building was put up in its place two years later. Has the Flapper Ghost simply moved on to the other side since her favorite dance spot has disappeared? Perhaps—and perhaps she is still kicking up her heels on a dance floor in another time and place, where it's 1933 every day!

Yet another phantom hitcher is said to haunt the roadways near Evergreen Cemetery in Evergreen Park, a Chicago suburb. For more than two decades, an attractive young teenage girl has been seen roaming out beyond the confines of the cemetery in search of a ride. A number of drivers claim to have spotted her, and in the 1980s, a flurry of encounters occurred when motorists in the south and western suburbs reported picking up this young girl. She always asked them for a ride to a location in Evergreen Park, and then mysteriously vanished from the vehicle at the cemetery.

According to the legends, she is the spirit of a child buried within the cemetery, but there is no real folklore to explain why she leaves her grave in search of travelers to bring her back home again. She is what some would call the typical vanishing hitchhiker, but there is one aspect to this ghost that sets her apart from the others: In addition to seeking rides in cars, she is resourceful enough to find other transportation when it suits her.

In recent years, encounters with this phantom have also taken place at a bus stop that is located directly across the street from the cemetery. Many have claimed to see a dark-haired young girl here who mysteriously vanishes. On occasion, she also has been witnessed climbing aboard a few Chicago Transit Authority buses.

One evening, a young girl boarded a bus and breezed right past the driver without paying the fare. She walked to the back portion of the vehicle and sat down, seemingly without a care in the world. Irritated, the driver called out to her, but she didn't answer. Finally he stood up and walked back toward where she was seating. She would either pay, he thought, or have to get off the bus. But before he could reach her, she vanished before his eyes.

According to reports, other shaken drivers have had the same eerie experience at this bus stop. They have also seen this young girl, and every single one of them has seen her disappear as if she had never been there in the first place.

RESURRECTION MARY

Chicago is a city seemingly filled with ghosts, from haunted houses to ghostly graveyards. But of all the tales, there is one spirit that rises above the others. Her name is Resurrection Mary, and she is Chicago's most famous ghost.

Mary's tale begins in the middle 1930s, when drivers along Archer Avenue on the city's Southwest Side began reporting that a young woman was attempting to jump onto the running boards of their automobiles as they passed by Resurrection Cemetery, a local Catholic burial ground.

Not long after, the woman became more mysterious and much more alluring. The strange encounters began to move farther away from the graveyard and closer to the Oh Henry Ballroom, which is now known as the Willowbrook. People reported seeing her on the nearby roadway and sometimes even inside the ballroom. On many occasions, young men would meet a girl at the ballroom, dance with her, and then offer her a ride home at the end of the evening. She would always accept and offer vague directions that would lead north on Archer Avenue. When the car reached the gates of Resurrection Cemetery, the young woman would always vanish.

Others had even more harrowing experiences. Rather than having the girl vanish from their cars, they claimed they ran her down in the street. But when they stopped to go to her aid, she would be gone. Some even said that the automobile passed directly through the girl. At that point, she would turn and disappear through the cemetery gates.

Bewildered and shaken drivers began to appear almost routinely in nearby businesses and even at the nearby police station. They told strange and frightening stories, and sometimes they were believed and sometimes they weren't. Regardless, they created an even greater legend of the vanishing girl, who became known as Resurrection Mary.

But who was this young woman when she was alive?

According to the legend, Resurrection Mary was a young woman who died on Archer Avenue in the early 1930s. She spent the evening dancing with her boyfriend at the Oh Henry Ballroom, and then, after an argument, left and began walking home. It was a cold winter's night, and a passing car slid on the ice and struck and killed her along the roadway. Her grieving parents buried her in Resurrection Cemetery, and since that time, her spirit has been seen along Archer Avenue, perhaps trying to return to her grave after one last night among the living.

This legend has been told and retold over the years, and it may just have some elements of the truth to it. As it turns out, though, there may be more than one Resurrection Mary haunting Archer Avenue.

One of the prime candidates for Mary's real-life identity was a young Polish girl named Marie Bregovy. Marie loved to dance, especially at the Oh Henry Ballroom, and was killed one night in March 1934 after spending the evening at the ballroom and then downtown at some of the late-night clubs. She was killed along Wacker Drive when the car she was riding in collided with an elevated train support. Her parents buried her in Resurrection Cemetery, and a short time later, a cemetery caretaker claimed to have spotted her ghost walking through the graveyard. Stranger still, passing motorists on Archer Avenue soon began telling stories of her ghost trying to hitch rides as they passed by the cemetery's front gates. For this reason, many believe that the ghost stories of Marie Bregovy may have given birth to the legend of Resurrection Mary.

But she may not be the only one. As encounters with Mary have been passed along over the years, many of the descriptions of the phantom have varied. Marie Bregovy had bobbed, light brown hair, but some reports of Mary describe an attractive blond. Who could this ghost be?

It's possible that this Mary may be a young woman named Mary Miskowski, who was killed along Archer Avenue in October 1930. According to sources, she also loved to dance at the Oh Henry Ballroom and some of the local night spots. Many people who knew her in life believed that she might be the ghostly hitchhiker reported all over the Southwest Side.

In the end, we may never know, but there is no denying that the story of Resurrection Mary has elements that other tales of vanishing hitchhikers do not—credible eyewitness accounts, places, times, and dates. Many of these reports are not just stories that have been passed from person to person and rely on a "friend of a friend" for authenticity. In fact, some of the encounters with Mary have been chillingly up close and personal, and they remain unexplained to this day. Besides that, Mary is one of the few ghosts ever to leave physical evidence behind.

This strange event occurred on the night of August 10, 1976. A driver was passing by the cemetery around 10:30 p.m. when he happened to see a girl standing on the other side of the gates. He said that when he saw her, she was wearing a white dress and grasping the iron bars of the gate. The driver was considerate enough to stop down the street at the Justice police station and alert them to the fact that someone had been accidentally locked in the cemetery at closing time. A patrolman named Pat Homa responded to the call, but when he arrived at the cemetery gates, he couldn't find anyone there. He called out with his loudspeaker and looked for her with his spotlight, but there was no one to be seen. He finally got out of his patrol car and walked up to the gates for one last look. As far as he could tell, the cemetery was dark and deserted, and there was no sign of any girl.

But his inspection of the gates, where the girl had been seen standing, did reveal something unusual. What he saw there chilled him to the bone! He found that two of the bronze bars in the gate had been blackened, burned, and—well, pulverized. It looked as though someone had taken two of the green-colored bars in his or her hands and had somehow just squashed and twisted them. Within the marks was what looked to be skin texture and handprints that had

HAUNTED ILLINOIS

been seared into the metal with incredible heat. The temperature, which must have been intense, blackened and burned the bars at just about the spot where a small woman's hands would have been.

The marks of the hands made big news, and curiosity seekers came from all over the area to see them. In an effort to discourage the crowds, cemetery officials attempted to remove the marks with a blowtorch, making them look even worse. Finally they cut the bars out of the gate and installed a wire fence until the two bars could be straightened or replaced.

The cemetery emphatically denied the supernatural version of what happened to the bars. In 1992, they claimed that a truck had backed into the gates while doing sewer work at the cemetery, and that grounds workers tried to fix the bars by heating them with a blowtorch and bending them. The imprint in the metal, they said, was from a workman trying to push them together again. Though this explanation was quite convenient, it did not explain why the marks of small fingers were clearly visible in the metal, or why the bronze never reverted to its green, oxidized state.

Though the bars were removed to discourage onlookers, taking them out actually had the opposite effect. Soon people began asking what the cemetery had to hide. The events allegedly embarrassed local officials, so they demanded that the bars be put back into place. Once they were returned to the gate, they were straightened and left alone so that the blackened areas would oxidize to match the other bars. Unfortunately, though, the scorched areas continued to defy nature, and the twisted spots where the handprints had been impressed remained obvious until just a few years ago, when the bars were finally removed for good. At great expense, Resurrection Cemetery replaced the entire front gates, and the notorious bars vanished for good.

Even though sightings and encounters have slacked off in recent years, they still continue to occur today. Though many of the stories are harder to believe these days, as the tales of Mary have infiltrated our culture to such a degree that almost anyone with an interest in ghosts has heard of her, some of the stories still appear to be chillingly real.

So does Mary really exist? I believe that she does, and I also believe that we know the identities of at least two of the girls who have created her enduring legend. But there are many other theories that also exist. Besides Mary Bregovy and Mary Miskowski, there may be many more.

Many still remain doubtful about her existence, but I have found that their skepticism doesn't really seem to matter. Whether these people believe in her or not, other people still report seeing Mary walking along Archer Avenue at night. Motorists are still stopping to pick up a forlorn figure that seems inadequately dressed on cold winter nights, when encounters seem to be the most prevalent. Curiosity seekers still come to see the gates where the twisted and burned bars were once located, and some even roam the graveyard, hoping to stumble across the place where Mary's body was laid to rest.

We still don't know for sure who she really was, but that has not stopped the stories from being told and even songs from being sung about her. She remains an enigma and her legend lives on, not content to vanish as Mary does when she reaches the gates to Resurrection Cemetery. You see, our individual belief, or disbelief, does not really matter. Mary lives on anyway—a mysterious, elusive, and romantic spirit of the Windy City.

RECOMMENDED READING

Adams, Joseph. "A Lost Village." *Historic Illinois*, August 1999.

Allen, John. *Legends and Lore of Southern Illinois*. Carbondale, IL: Southern Illinois University Press, 1963.

Asbury, Herbert. *Gem of the Prairie*. New York: Alfred A. Knopf, 1940.

Banton, O. T. *History of Macon County, Illinois*. Decatur, IL: Macon County Historical Society, 1976.

Bettenhausen, Brad. "Batchelor Grove Cemetery." *Where the Trails Cross* newsletter, 1995.

Bielski, Ursula. *Chicago Haunts*. Chicago: Lake Claremont Press, 1998.

Cowdery, Ray. *Capone's Chicago*. Lakeville, MN: Northstar Commemoratives, 1987.

Crowe, Richard. *Chicago's Street Guide to the Supernatural*. Chicago: Carolando Press, 2000.

Davis, James E. *Frontier Illinois*. Bloomington, IN: Indiana University Press, 1998.

Donald, David Herbert. *Lincoln*. New York: Simon & Shuster, 1995.

Drury, John. "Old Illinois Houses." *Fate Magazine* (various issues). Springfield, IL: Illinois State Historical Society, 1948.

Fliege, Stu. *Tales & Trails of Illinois*. Urbana, IL: University of Illinois Press, 2002.

Howard, Robert. *Illinois: A History of the Prairie State*. Grand Rapids, MI: William B. Eerdman's Publishing, 1972.

Kaczmarek, Dale. *Windy City Ghosts*. Alton, IL: Whitechapel Press, 2000.

———. *Windy City Ghosts* II. Alton, IL: Whitechapel Press, 2001.

Kobler, John. *Capone*. New York: G. P. Putman's Sons, 1971.

Lewis, Lloyd. *Myths After Lincoln*. New York: Harcourt, Brace & Co., 1929.

Lindberg, Richard. *Chicago by Gaslight*. Chicago: Chicago Academy Publishers, 1996.

Magee, Judy. *Cavern of Crime*. Smithland, KY. Livingston Ledger, 1973.

Neely, Charles. *Tales and Songs of Southern Illinois*. Menasha, WI: George Banta Publishing Company, 1938.

Norman, Michael, and Beth Scott. *Haunted America*. New York: Tor, 1994.

———. *Historic Haunted America*. New York: Tor, 1995.

Parrish, Randall. *Historic Illinois*. Chicago: A. C. McClurg & Co., 1905.

Quaife, Milo. *Chicago Highways Old and New*. Chicago: D.F. Keller & Co., 1923.

Rothert, Otto. *Outlaws of Cave-in-Rock*. Cleveland: A. H. Clark & Co., 1924.

Russell, Dorotha. *Squire of Voorhies*. Monticello, IL: Illinois Pioneer Heritage Center, 1967.

St. Clair, David. *Watseka*. Chicago: Playboy Press, 1977.

Scott, Beth, and Michael Norman. *Haunted Heartland*. New York: Dorset Press, 1985.

Taylor, Troy. *Ghosts of the Prairie*. Jacksonville, IL: American Hauntings Ink, 2016

———. *Haunted Alton*. Alton, IL: Whitechapel Press, 2000 and 2003.

———. *Haunted Chicago*. Alton, IL: Whitechapel Press, 2002.

———. *Haunted Decatur*. Decatur, IL: Whitechapel Press, 2006.

———. *Haunted Illinois*. Alton, IL: Whitechapel Press, 2004.

———. *Haunted President*. Decatur, IL: Whitechapel Press, 2005.

———. *In the Boneyard*. Jacksonville, IL: American Hauntings Ink, 2020.

———. *Resurrection Mary*. Decatur, IL: Whitechapel Press, 2007.

Winer, Richard, and Nancy Osborn Ishmael. *More Haunted Houses*. New York: Bantam, 1981.

ABOUT THE AUTHOR

Troy Taylor is the author of more than 125 books about history, hauntings, true crime, and the unexplained in America. He is the founder of American Hauntings Ink, which offers books, events, and tours about haunted history. In addition to writing about the macabre and hosting tours, Taylor is a public speaker and has been quoted in newspaper and magazine articles about ghosts and has been interviewed hundreds of times for radio and television broadcasts about the supernatural. He has also appeared in a number of documentary films, several television series, and one feature film about the paranormal. He currently resides in Central Illinois.